MARY IN THE CHRISTIAN TRADITION

Mary in the Christian Tradition

Owen F. Cummings

Paulist Press
New York / Mahwah, NJ

The Scripture quotations contained herein are from the New Revised Standard Version: Catholic Edition, Copyright © 1989 and 1993, by the Division of Christian Education of the National Council of the Churches of Christ in the United States of America. Used by permission. All rights reserved.

Cover image by agsandrew/Shutterstock.com
Cover and book design by Lynn Else

Copyright © 2022 by Owen F. Cummings

All rights reserved. No part of this publication may be reproduced, stored in a retrieval system, or transmitted in any form or by any means, electronic, mechanical, photocopying, recording, scanning, or otherwise, without either the prior written permission of the Publisher, or authorization through payment of the appropriate per-copy fee to the Copyright Clearance Center, Inc., www.copyright.com. Requests to the Publisher for permission should be addressed to the Permissions Department, Paulist Press, permissions@paulistpress.com.

Library of Congress Cataloging-in-Publication Data
Names: Cummings, Owen F, author.
Title: Mary in the Christian tradition / Owen F. Cummings.
Description: New York / Mahwah, NJ : Paulist Press, [2022] | Includes bibliographical references. | Summary: "Owen Cummings provides an overview of Mary in the Christian tradition, beginning with the New Testament, through the Reformation, and finishing up with contemporary views on her role"—Provided by publisher.
Identifiers: LCCN 2021032139 (print) | LCCN 2021032140 (ebook) | ISBN 9780809155897 (paperback) | ISBN 9781587689925 (ebook)
Subjects: LCSH: Mary, Blessed Virgin, Saint—History of doctrines.
Classification: LCC BT610 .C86 2022 (print) | LCC BT610 (ebook) | DDC 232.91—dc23
LC record available at https://lccn.loc.gov/2021032139
LC ebook record available at https://lccn.loc.gov/2021032140

ISBN 978-0-8091-5589-7 (paperback)
ISBN 978-1-58768-992-5 (e-book)

Published by Paulist Press
997 Macarthur Boulevard
Mahwah, New Jersey 07430
www.paulistpress.com

Printed and bound in the
United States of America

CONTENTS

Preface vii
1. The Historical Mary of Nazareth 1
2. Images of Mary in the New Testament 15
3. Patristic Mary 38
4. Syriac Mary 51
5. Celtic Mary 57
6. Muslim Mary 65
7. Medieval Mary 73
8. Mary and the Reformers 80
9. Mary in Vatican II's Constitution on the Church 90
10. The Marian Dogmas 96
11. At the School of Mary, "Woman of the Eucharist" .. 108
12. Praying the Rosary 120
13. Mary Today 131
Notes 141
Bibliography 161

PREFACE

This little book on our Blessed Lady is not intended to be a work of serious academic theology, although it is not absent of academic insight and the wisdom of so many scholars. Rather, it hopes to be of use to mediate an informed perspective on Mary for contemporary Catholics interested in developing their understanding of their faith.

I have been interested in the theology of Mary for many years, and one of my earliest essays in exploring Christian doctrine had to do with the immaculate conception.[1] Over the years, that interest has remained and has resulted in several published reflections on our Blessed Lady. Now I am trying to pull together these various Marian interests into a contemporary statement that I hope will be helpful to other adult Catholics, and perhaps interested others.

Chapter 1 attempts to reconstruct something of the historical Mary, what we know about her as a historical person. There are almost no data on which to go, but by using the work of some contemporary scholars on women in Second Temple Judaism, and especially the first century of Christianity, I hope to have provided some possible background to some aspects of Mary's life. Moving on from there, in chapter 2 consideration is given over to various theological images and portraits of Mary in the New Testament and especially the Gospels. In chapters 3 and 4 we move into the post-New Testament period with a consideration of selected patristic authors—Greek, Latin, and Syriac. This is followed by chapter 5, with a brief consideration of Mary in Celtic theology. Celtic reflections on Mary originated during the patristic era with the advent of St. Patrick, a contemporary of St. Augustine, but did not find written expression until later. They provide an interesting contrast to the more developed Marian theology of the Mediterranean and Middle Eastern areas. Chapter 6 takes up what I call "Muslim Mary." Most Catholics are simply unaware of the high regard in which Mary is held in traditional Islam and this chapter tries to fill the gap, albeit briefly. Mary in the medieval period and the Reformation period forms the substance of chapters 7 and 8. Marian theology flourished in the Middle Ages, and undoubtedly it was the populist flourishing of devotion to our Lady that was one of the many complex factors in bringing about the Reformation of the sixteenth century. It may come as something of a surprise to Catholics that the thinkers of the sixteenth century who sought to reform the Church had their own understanding of and devotion to Mary. However, they came about it with respect to their own theological principles, as we will see. Mary in Vatican II's Constitution on the Church and the two Marian dogmas of the immaculate conception and the assumption are dealt with in chapters 9 and 10. The intention is to underscore that these two dogmas should not speak exclusively with regard to Mary but that they also have to do with the Church, that is, ourselves. Pope St. John Paul II provided an attractive interpretation of Mary and the Eucharist, and this is the subject of chapter 11. Chapter 12 attempts to explore the mysteries of the Rosary, and chapter 13, entitled "Mary Today," seeks to understand the position of Mary in the rather broad terms of modern attitudes and suggests ways of retrieving devotion to Mary today.

Preface

It will be obvious to the reader that I am reliant upon the work of countless scholars—historians and theologians, past and present. Each generation stands on the shoulders of those who have gone before it. I have attempted to acknowledge these authors at the end in the bibliography. If this popular presentation of Marian theology in snapshots leads people to a better understanding and to a greater devotion to Mary, the author will be well pleased.

1

THE HISTORICAL MARY OF NAZARETH

> Our knowledge about [Mary's] history as a specific human person may be minimal. But we are now in a position to draw a concrete picture of the world she inhabited and to allow this picture to shape our imaginations of the warp and woof of her life.
>
> Elizabeth A. Johnson, CSJ[1]

> It is entirely logical to deduce that the historical Mary had an important and pivotal role to play, not only on the formation of Jesus himself but also in the development of the Jesus movement after him.
>
> John A. McGuckin[2]

DE-HISTORICIZING AND DE-HUMANIZING MIRIAM

When you care about someone, especially when you love that person, you want to know all about them. Even a casual awareness of the theological and devotional texts of the Christian tradition, both prose and poetry, as well as the artistic representations concerning Mary, the mother of Jesus, will demonstrate to the observer just how much the figure of Mary means to Christians over two millennia and how much they love her. At the same time, one might also observe that as the Christian tradition develops there is a tendency to magnify Mary in a way that is entirely appropriate to devotion, but unfortunately that magnification may underplay something of her actual historicity. One commentator has written that "in trying to go far back beyond the texts to reconstruct the life of the individual woman Mary of Nazareth in any academic historical sense, one has very few resources; the task is impossible."[3] That is correct. While we have no direct access whatsoever to the historical Mary and to historical details about her life—her background, her birth, her parents—we can say two things about her without qualification: that she was a Palestinian peasant, and that she was a Jewess.

She was a Palestinian peasant. That is not how she is represented, however, in the texts and artwork of the later Christian tradition. Later Christians, it might be said, had little use for a Mary understood as a Palestinian peasant. The biblical scholar John L. McKenzie makes this point very well:

> One may venture a bit further and assert that the needs [of the tenth to the seventeenth centuries] felt by the ruling classes of Christendom which patronized the art and the literature of those centuries [were not for a Palestinian peasant woman]. The mere reality of a first century Palestinian village housewife obviously met none of these devotional needs, because that is not what the poems, hymns, art, and legends represented. About Palestinian housewives they knew nothing; if they had, they would have found her like the maids of

The Historical Mary of Nazareth

their palace kitchens or the peasant women of their domains. They were not going to hang pictures of these humble, common folk on their walls, or sing hymns praising their virtue and beauty. Before they could venerate Mary, they had to make her one of themselves; that is, they had to destroy her.[4]

In my judgment, McKenzie is going a little too far in saying that our ancestors in the faith had to destroy Mary, but he surely is correct in recognizing that their devotion to her found expression in cultural forms that were able to speak to their immediate experience. That experience would have been enriched had they been able to retrieve something of Mary's Palestinian peasant background, but surely not destroyed because that retrieval was impossible for them.

Mary was a Jewess. This fact was easily forgotten as Christianity morphed into Christendom, becoming the major religion of the West. The parting of the ways between Judaism and Christianity that began in the late first century CE, and continued thereafter, grew into hostile rivalry and outright persecution. This can be documented without difficulty in any standard account of the history of Western Christianity. The West forgot in many ways that Jesus was a Jew, and that Mary was a Jewess. The Jewish New Testament scholar Amy-Jill Levine puts it accurately when she says,

> Today Jesus's words are too familiar, too domesticated, too stripped of their initial edginess and urgency. Only when heard through first-century Jewish ears can their original edginess and urgency be recovered. Consequently, to understand the man from Nazareth, it is necessary to understand Judaism. More, it is necessary to see Jesus as firmly within Judaism rather than as standing apart from

it, and it is essential that the picture of Judaism not be distorted through the filter of centuries of Christian stereotypes.[5]

Reading the details of what happened to the Jews at the hands of Christians through the centuries makes very sad reading indeed. Trying to rediscover anew the Jewishness of Jesus, and one might add the Jewishness of Mary, is one of the achievements of contemporary theological scholarship. One scholar makes the point through a number of uncomfortable questions: "Would there have been such anti-Semitism, would there have been so many pogroms, would there have been an Auschwitz, if every Christian church and every Christian home had focused its devotions on icons of Mary not only as Mother of God and Queen of Heaven, but as the Jewish maiden and the new Miriam, and on icons of Christ not only as Pantocrator but as Rabbi Jeshua bar-Joseph, Rabbi Jesus of Nazareth?"[6]

THE HISTORICAL MIRIAM OF NAZARETH

Trying to describe the context in life of Mary in the first half of the first century CE is no easy task. We have no immediate sources other than the texts of the New Testament. When it comes to Jewish sources, the Mishnah and the Talmud, immediately we come up against a problem. While undoubtedly the information and the traditions found in these sources reflect what was the case in the first century, in point of fact we have no way of verifying this. The challenge of our Jewish sources is well put by Tai Ilan. "[These documents] posit an ideal society, and many of their rulings may hint more at behavior they wish to encourage or to combat than at

The Historical Mary of Nazareth

standards currently practiced. At the same time, these works are not directly concerned with history or historical inquiry."[7] Even with this important caveat, however, the desire to understand something more about Miriam compels us to press on. We have to proceed then on an "as if" basis. If we can trust these Jewish sources as reflecting first-century traditions, "as if" they were providing us with an accurate understanding, then we may be able to reconstruct something of what the life of Miriam of Nazareth may have been like.

I am following in the main the work of the University of Cambridge Jewish scholar Rabbi Nicholas de Lange.[8] The Torah is clearly centrally important for a Jew, and so what would the Torah have meant in terms of practical implications for a first-century Galilean Jewish woman? Probably the passage in the Torah that comes to most people's minds is the beautiful prayer from the Book of Deuteronomy, the Shema.

> Hear, O Israel! The Lord is our God, the Lord alone. You shall love the Lord your God with all your heart and with all your soul and with all your might. Take to heart these instructions with which I charge you this day. Impress them upon your children. Recite them when you stay at home and when you are away, when you lie down and when you get up. Bind them as a sign on your hand and let them serve as a symbol on your forehead; inscribe them on the doorposts of your house and on your gates. (Deut 6:4–9)

It would be a misunderstanding to interpret all the many instructions of the Torah as a legalistic way of understanding or expressing Jewish relationship with God. It is loving God that is the basis of Torah observance and the Book of Deuteronomy in which the Shema appears is "the biblical book of the love of God par excellence."⁹ Where did Mary stand in relation to Torah observance? She obviously loved God, but in terms of the various commandments with regard to women, Rabbi de Lange explains that in the 613 commandments of the Torah, 365 of them were in the form of prohibitions and 248 in the form of positive commands. Women were to keep all the prohibitions and the positive commands that had no time specification, the latter being important because of the time of menstruation, which would have rendered a woman ritually unclean. Because of this maintains de Lange, the biologically necessary incomplete observance of all the commandments on a woman's part made her somewhat inferior to a man. Thus, men thanked God "for not making me a woman," but women thanked God "for making me according to your will."¹⁰ When it came to attendance in the temple in Jerusalem, women were not given a full part to play in public worship and were restricted to the Court of the Women. On the other hand, there is evidence according to de Lange that women attended the local synagogues not only on the Sabbath day and festivals but also during the week.¹¹ While the Gospel of St. Luke (2:22–50) mentions Miriam attending the temple, there is no such mention of her attending the Sabbath service in the synagogue. That does not mean that she was absent, but simply that we have no record of it, although it seems very likely that as a devout Jewish woman she would have been regularly in attendance.

Was Miriam educated? Was she literate? Later Christian artistry shows Miriam on the occasion of the annunciation reading a book, but that seems not to have been the case historically. Some rabbis thought that teaching girls to read, and so to read the Torah, was to be avoided—"To teach a daughter Torah is tantamount to teaching her lechery"¹²—while other rabbis educated their daughters as they did their sons. What was the case with Miriam of Nazareth? The likelihood is that she was illiterate but far from ignorant. She may not have been able to read or write, but in educational terms there was so much more to her than that.

What about the married Jewish woman? It seems to have been the case that a woman in first-century Judaism was largely under the control of her father until marriage, when she passed under the control of her husband in clearly a patriarchal society. "Men, as a general rule, owned women's reproductive capacities. The transactions they conducted concerned the acquisition of these capacities by the husband from the father. Women were thus treated as chattels."[13] Marriages may often have been arranged, but Rabbi de Lange points out that by the first century CE a Jewish woman was sufficiently free of parental control as to be able to choose her husband.[14] Marriage was a two-stage process, stage one being betrothal, which was as binding as marriage itself, although the couple did not actually live together, and stage two, about one year later, when the young woman moved from her parental home to her husband's family home. If these customs and traditions pertained to Miriam, then she may have been about fourteen or fifteen years of age when betrothed to Joseph, and he would have been about eighteen years old. Jewish men were expected to marry by about eighteen years of age and hopefully to have fathered a son by the end of the first year of marriage.[15] As with Miriam, we know so little about Joseph from the pages of the Gospels. He is quite literally without a voice in the texts, and after the infancy narratives he never appears at all. The supposition is that Joseph died quite early. Based on that supposition, I find the words of theologian Elizabeth Johnson both interesting and moving. This is what she writes:

> Was Mary cast into deepest grief at his death, or resigned, or relieved, or filled with ambiguous feelings of all three? We will never know. Some thinkers

point to the loving, compassionate qualities of the adult Jesus and deduce that his character would be most likely to emerge from a household of the same caliber—the apple does not fall far from the tree. Others speculate that in simple human terms Joseph, whom the historical child Jesus would have literally called *Abba*, served as the concrete reference for the gracious God of compassion whom Jesus called by the same name.[16]

ST. JOSEPH OF NAZARETH

If we know so little about the historical Miriam of Nazareth, we know just as little about her husband the historical St. Joseph. Joseph was a common name in Judaism of the first century CE after the Patriarch Joseph, son of Jacob. Outside the infancy narratives of the Gospels of St. Matthew and St. Luke we have just a handful of incidental references to Joseph. In Matthew 13:55 he is not named but is described as "the carpenter." In Luke 3:23 Joseph is named as the "supposed" father of Jesus. In John 1:45 the same point is made as Jesus is described as the "son of Joseph." The same description is made in John 6:42.

Matthew 13:55 describes Joseph as a *tekton*, a "woodworker," or "carpenter" (see also Mark 6:3). He probably worked hard for a living, but it does not seem that the holy family would have lived necessarily in grinding poverty. Sepphoris, Herod's new capital city of Galilee, was a well-to-do city, a city that would have offered plenty of work to a woodworker/carpenter, and it was just a few miles from Nazareth. We should probably imagine Joseph, perhaps accompanied by Jesus, working regularly in Sepphoris. Joseph would probably not only have taught Jesus his own trade of *tekton*, but

The Historical Mary of Nazareth

also something of the religious traditions and texts of Judaism because, as Msgr. John P. Meier, the premier Catholic scholar of the historical Jesus, puts it, Jesus certainly had "a reading knowledge imparted either directly by Joseph or by some more learned Jew procured for the purpose."[17] The Jewish historian Geza Vermes speculates a little more on Joseph as a carpenter. He makes the point that the terms *carpenter* and *son of a carpenter* are used in the Talmud to indicate a learned man. Though Vermes recognizes that it is impossible to be absolutely sure that the sayings in the Talmud were already in circulation in first-century Galilee, nonetheless he concludes that such connections may be age-old, and so he posits the possibility that a description of Joseph as *naggar*, the Hebrew word for "carpenter," might indicate that he was considered wise and well versed in the Torah.[18] If that were so, Joseph would have been in an excellent position to tradition his Judaism to Jesus.

"Art and popular imagination have usually pictured Joseph as an old man. But this is surely a false idea."[19] This description of Joseph as an old man is widespread. One example from a recent novel by P. D. James, as she describes a painting of the holy family is as follows:

> Mary was seated on a low stool with the naked Christ child resting on a white cloth on her lap. Her face was a pale and perfect oval, the mouth tender under a narrow nose, the heavily lidded eyes under thinly arced brows fixed on the child with an expression of resigned wonder. From a high smooth forehead the strands of crimped auburn hair fell over her blue mantle to the delicate hands and fingers barely touching in prayer. The child gazed up at her with both hands raised, as if foreshadowing the crucifixion. St. Joseph, red-coated, was seated to the right

in the painting, a prematurely aged, half-sleeping custodian, heavily leaning on a stick.[20]

The depiction of Joseph as an old man is almost certainly wrong. The rabbis at the time taught that a man should be married about the age of eighteen, and one may take it as reasonably certain that was Joseph's age when he was engaged to Mary, the mother of Jesus. The image of Joseph as an older man comes from the mid-second-century apocryphal text *The Protoevangelium of James*. In this immensely influential text, "a wildly imaginative folk narrative," Joseph is portrayed as an older man, as a widower with children by his previous wife.[21] The author of this text is seeking to protect the notion of Mary's virginity, and so not only is Joseph portrayed as up in years, but also as having had children by a former marriage, thus accounting for the references in the Gospels to "the brothers of Jesus." Whether or not this was the case historically, it is impossible to know.

The only other information about Joseph comes from Matthew 1—2, and Luke 1—2, the infancy narratives. Without getting into complex questions of historicity, we may note with Msgr. John P. Meier the peculiarity of these narratives. "Even in these two Gospels, events in the Infancy Narratives are almost never referred to once chapter 3 of each Gospel is reached. Thus, within Matthew and Luke themselves, the Infancy Narratives stand in relative isolation; they are distinct compositions stemming from traditions different from those found elsewhere in the Four Gospels—and indeed in the rest of the New Testament."[22] These observations by Meier should make us somewhat cautious in approaching the historicity of these texts. All serious scholars agree that the two narratives ought not to be conflated. Matthew and Luke have their own theological contributions to make, independently of one another. Joseph features prominently in Matthew, but only marginally in Luke.

Apart from Jesus himself, the central character in Matthew's infancy narrative is Joseph. We learn that he is betrothed to Mary. Betrothal meant more than "engagement" in our sense, but less than complete marriage, as we have seen. It consisted of a formal contract that made the man and woman husband and wife. A betrothal ceremony took place at the home of the father of the bride. Mary would have remained in her parents' home, and Joseph would have visited her from time to time until they came to live together as husband and wife. Conjugal infidelity on the part of the "betrothed" woman was regarded as adultery. The betrothal ceremony was followed after several months by the actual wedding, the ceremony by which the man received the woman into his house and consummated the marriage.

In Matthew 1:18–25, we are told that Joseph noticed that Mary was pregnant, while she was "betrothed" to him. He was a "just" man, that is, an observant and pious Jew. The Torah did not allow him to consummate marriage with a woman who had been guilty of adultery during the period of betrothal. According to Deuteronomy 22:22–23, a woman who is betrothed but sleeps with another man is to be stoned to death. It is not clear how widespread this punishment was in the first century CE. From the text it seems that Joseph intended to put Mary through the much less public procedure of divorce. This is in line with an injunction of the Mishnah: "If she says, 'I am defiled,' she forfeits her marriage contract and goes forth."[23] After the revelation from God in a dream, Joseph "took Mary as wife," that is, they went through with the second marital ceremony, the wedding. "He knew her not until she had borne a son" (Matt 1:25). The purpose of the statement is to insist on Mary's virginity at the time of Jesus's conception.

MARY IN THE CHRISTIAN TRADITION

The Catholic doctrine of the perpetual virginity of Mary goes back to the very early Church, but it is not formally and explicitly implied in this statement from the Gospel. The reference to the "brothers and sisters" of Jesus in Matthew 12:46–50; 13:55–56 is inconclusive with respect to actual siblings. It is simply a philological fact that the term "brothers and sisters" could and did refer not only to children of the same mother and father, but also to other relatives.

Nowhere is Joseph mentioned as present during the public ministry of Jesus. The supposition is that he had died by that time, almost certainly before he was fifty years of age. That premier pursuer of the historical Jesus, John P. Meier, writes,

> Granted that we do not know how old Joseph was when Jesus was born, and granted that life expectancy was much lower in the ancient world than in the United States today, there is nothing intrinsically improbable about Joseph's death before Jesus reached the age of roughly thirty to thirty-five....In contrast, Mary lived through the public ministry and on into at least the early days of the Church.... She would have been roughly forty-eight to fifty years old at the time of his crucifixion.[24]

In the Office of Readings from March 19, the Church lays before us an extract from a sermon by the Franciscan St. Bernardine of Siena (1380–1444):

> There is a general rule concerning all special graces granted to any human being. Whenever the divine favor chooses someone to receive a special grace, or to accept a lofty vocation, God adorns the person

chosen with all the gifts of the Spirit needed to fulfill the task at hand. This general rule is especially verified in the case of St. Joseph, the foster-father of our Lord and the husband of the Queen of our world, enthroned above the angels....Holy Church in its entirety is indebted to the Virgin Mother because through her it was judged worthy to receive Christ. But after her we undoubtedly owe special gratitude to St. Joseph. In him the Old Testament finds its fitting close. He brought the noble line of patriarchs and prophets to its promise to fulfillment. What the divine goodness had offered as a promise to them, he held in his arms.

St. Joseph wrote nothing and said nothing that is recorded in the Gospels. Perhaps we might say that Joseph, equipped by the Spirit, was *pre-evangelized* by doing the things that he had to do to look after Jesus, to stand by and support his wife and her child. His witness was one of deed, not word. Through the choices he made, and following through on those choices, he fulfilled the promises made to the patriarchs and the prophets, that is to say, he "filled full" in his custody of Jesus and in his nurturing of Jesus, the incarnational aspirations of the Old Testament.

CONCLUSION

As we conclude this chapter, we should say a word about Nazareth. Nazareth was so insignificant to all except to the two or three hundred people who lived there that it never even merited a mention in the Hebrew Bible. A few miles north of Nazareth, however, lay the garrison town of Sepphoris, a new city, and it may be the case as we have noted that Joseph the carpenter found work there.

Putting together this admittedly hypothetical material when it comes to Miriam, we get a "picture" of Miriam of Nazareth. At the time of Jesus's birth, she may have been about sixteen years old. She was inferior to her husband Joseph according to Jewish tradition, and though probably a regular worshiper in the synagogue, she was herself unable to read. What did she look like? She would have been like the majority of Palestinian women, dark-skinned and slight of stature.[25]

2

IMAGES OF MARY IN THE NEW TESTAMENT

Both on the ecumenical level and in terms of popular devotion, I think that modern insight into the Scriptures is very productive and loyal to the best traditions of mariology.

Raymond E. Brown[1]

When we look at Mary, we are looking at our own mystery, looking at a mirror in which we see ourselves, different and distinct from each of us as she is. We see the Church in Mary and Mary in the Church.

Geoffrey Preston, OP[2]

In meeting Mary anew, men meet a part of themselves that they need to own. She offers men the opportunity to reclaim the motherly aspects of their own natures, just as she offers women the opportunity to reclaim their sense of autonomy and self-worth before God.

Tina Beattie[3]

MARY IN THE CHRISTIAN TRADITION

These three initial quotations help to provide direction for this chapter on "Images of Mary in the New Testament." First, Raymond Brown reminds us that we need not fear modern approaches to the interpretation of the Scriptures. In his judgment such modern approaches help to promote Christian unity and the best of Mariology, both key commitments for Catholics. Geoffrey Preston, an English Dominican and outstanding preacher, invites us to recognize ourselves as Church in our Lady and our Lady in the Church, and this will become a key insight for the understanding of our Blessed Lady in the documents of Vatican II and in the development of Marian theology afterward. Tina Beattie, a Catholic lay theologian and mother, indicates something of the gift that Mary may be for both women and men. They introduce this chapter on the New Testament Mary, or perhaps better, "Marys," to orient our reading and study. Combining biblical-theological interpretation with creative reflection, the aim is to look at Mary from various angles in order to better appreciate her role and place in Christian devotion and doctrine. It is particularly important because in the past the texts about Mary in the New Testament have been read somewhat selectively. A selective reading of the texts will inevitably lead to an unbalanced theological portrayal of Mary. Scripture scholar Raymond Brown, describing an ecumenical study group on Mary in the New Testament, once wrote,

> When we began to discuss which texts should be discussed first, some of the Protestants suggested that we should study the Marcan texts, while immediately some Catholics thought of the Lucan texts. I reflected that John McHugh's 500-page *The Mother of Jesus in the New Testament* had never seriously treated the basic Marcan text on Mary—a sign of just how alien Mark's voice on Mary was for

Catholics. Yet it also became obvious that some of our Protestant confrères had never really looked at the Lucan texts independently of Mark. Obviously we had to agree to look at all the Marian texts in the New Testament if we were to allow Scripture to challenge our divisive presuppositions.[4]

Brown's words stand as a warning to us. If we are to develop an adequate understanding of Mary from the various books of the New Testament, and especially from the Gospels, we need to do justice to all of the texts and not simply to those that have the most theological and devotional appeal for us.

AN ORDINARY JEWISH WOMAN (GAL 4:4)

But when the fullness of time had come, God sent his Son, born of a woman, born under the law.

St. Paul's letters are the oldest documents of the New Testament. In this passage referring to the birth of Jesus, Mary is not even named by St. Paul, something that Raymond Brown describes as "startling."[5] She is simply the woman who gives birth to God's Son, and she is a Jewish woman since that Son is "born under the law," that is to say born "under the Torah." From our point of view, it may seem that St. Paul marginalizes Mary in this verse, but that is not necessarily the case. Paul's primary focus throughout his letters is on the paschal mystery, the death and resurrection of Christ, and, because of this, he shows little interest in what we would call the "historical Jesus." What the passage tells us about our Lady may be minimal, but it is significant. It tells us that both Jesus and Mary are really human, "born of a woman," and that they were Jews. The New Testament scholar, Ben Witherington, writes, "Jesus was born of a woman, which simply conveys the idea that he was a normal human being, coming into the world in the normal way....What the phrase emphasizes is that Jesus was truly human. The phrase 'born under the Law' makes quite clear that Jesus was born a Jew...."[6] Mary is a Jewish woman, the kind of woman whose life situation was outlined in chapter 1.

Some scholars are inclined to say more, and I agree. A case can be made for holding the view that in this text St. Paul is also affirming the doctrine of Christ's preexistence. Emphasizing that Christ is "born of a woman" does not make much sense given the fact that that is how all humans are born. It does not tell us anything that we do not already know. That is, thinking along with Catholic theologian Lawrence Cunningham, "unless Paul understood Jesus to be someone distinguished from all other humans. In that stipulation, then, we can see (or better, we could argue) both the idea of pre-existence, albeit not developed, as well as 'a change of status that later theology would call the incarnation.' It is, in short, for the momentous character and significance of this person 'born of a woman' that the assertion is made."[7] That St. Paul may be referring, albeit obliquely, to the preexistence of Christ is just possible, not certain, in this passage.

MARY, THE PERPLEXED MOTHER (MARK 3:19b-21, 31-35)

The depiction of Mary in the Synoptic Gospels provide us only with "some brushstrokes," but brushstrokes worth attending to, not least in the somewhat strange references in the Gospel of St. Mark.[8]

Images of Mary in the New Testament

Then he went home with [the Twelve]; and the crowd came together again, so that they could not even eat. When his family heard it, they went out to restrain him, for people were saying, "He has gone out of his mind...." Then his mother and his brothers came; and standing outside, they sent to him and called him. A crowd was sitting around him; and they said to him, "Your mother and your brothers and sisters are outside asking for you." And he replied, "Who are my mother and my brothers?" And looking at those who sat around him, he said, "Here are my mother and my brothers! Whoever does the will of God is my brother and sister and mother." (Mark 3:19b–21, 31–35)

"Although Mark says very little about [Mary], what he says fits in so badly with what came to be the conventional view of Mary that it does have the ring of historical truth about it."[9] These words of the Anglican theologian John Macquarrie are surely correct. There is so obviously a certain tension here among Jesus, Mary, and the family that is not in harmony with what later came to be the normative view of our Lady, that it has all the feel of accurate historical recall. At the same time, Eamon Duffy, a Catholic theologian and church historian, points out that "this apparent hostility to Jesus' family reflects not a straightforward historical judgment about individuals, but an attitude towards the Judaic roots of the Christian movement, for...elsewhere in the New Testament Mary certainly does represent Israel."[10] The passage raises a number of questions for us. First, who are the brothers and sisters of Jesus? Are they his actual, biological siblings, children of Mary and Joseph? As has already been noted, it is quite impossible to answer this question absolutely from the text itself, from the language and vocabulary used. As Catholics, steeped in the tradition of Christian thinking over two thousand years, we accept the virginal conception of Jesus as part of God's gift-giving to humankind.[11] Most commentators in fact point out that "brothers and sisters" can mean in the context not only blood brothers and sisters, but also members of the extended family. The tradition of the Catholic Church, which there seems no good or compelling reason to dismiss, is that "brothers and sisters" do refer in some sense to this extended family of Jesus.

The second question raised by the passage has to do directly with Mary and what she knew of Jesus. The passage assumes a degree of tension, for want of a better word, between her and Jesus. One might ask, "What about the information and understanding Mary received from the angel Gabriel at the annunciation?" We need, in response to this question to recognize that there was no annunciation to Mary in St. Mark's Gospel, the Gospel with which we are dealing, and, therefore, within the frame of this Gospel, one ought not to assume any further knowledge or insight on our Lady's part than the text permits. John Macquarrie puts it nicely: "What we forget is that although we know the story of the annunciation, Mark did not know it, or certainly gives no indication of having known it."[12]

The third question is, "What does the phrase 'he is out of his mind' mean in this context?" Philologically it can only mean something like "He has gone mad or insane." That makes it is a very challenging statement from the point of view of Christian faith. It may be for that reason that the phrase has been omitted in the parallel passages of Matthew 12:12–32 and Luke 11:14–23. But perhaps we ought not to attribute more to it than the passage and especially the context actually warrant. It may be that St. Mark has used this phrase to lead to theological insight more than to report historical fact. "Its intent is more rhetorical than historical. It addresses and challenges all who view their Christian identity in terms of family, tribe, ethnicity or background. To read it as a historical statement about Jesus' relatives is to miss the point."[13] Ultimately, the passage is asking us how narrowly we define our Christian identity. In our self-definition as Christians—and we all operate out of some degree of self-definition—are we too much bound by family, tribe, ethnicity, or background? Pondering this issue is challenging, yes, but it also has the potential to lead to a much liberated and generous discipleship of Jesus.

Nevertheless, it still remains possible in this fascinating passage that Mary turns out to be a perplexed mother, a mother who is naturally anxious about her son. From her angle of vision in the Gospel of St. Mark, she does not understand or grasp the mission of Jesus, she is fearful of what might happen to him, and she wants to do what she can to help. "Mary's most obvious place in the christology of Mark remains bound up with the flesh and blood humanity of Jesus, this man of emotions, questions and limits. As mother, she is the cause of her son's humble state and she remains an inseparable part of that state."[14]

THE WIDOW (MARK 6:3)

> Is not this the carpenter, the son of Mary and brother of James and Joses and Judas and Simon?

Jesus is described as "son of Mary." Among the Jews, a man was called after his father. There is no mention of Joseph. Because explicit reference is made to other living relatives of Jesus, it seems likely that Joseph has died and Mary is a widow.[15] It is a very human image of Mary: a single parent, a widow, concerned about her son.

MARY IN THE CHRISTIAN TRADITION

The More Careful Matthew

In a very interesting essay on Mary in the Gospel of Matthew, New Testament scholar Beverly Gaventa examines the situations of the four women whose names occur in the genealogy in Matthew 1: Tamar (Gen 28), Rahab (Josh 6), Ruth (the Book of Ruth), and Bathsheba (2 Sam 11).[16] She points out that in a strongly patriarchal genealogy these women "whose stories teem with ambiguity and impropriety" stand out "as something like road signs within the text."[17] There is something ambiguous and improper from the sexual/marital point of view about each of the four women, perhaps anticipating the somewhat ambiguous and improper situation of Mary, who toward the end of that first chapter of Matthew is found to be with child but not by her husband, Joseph. In a sense, these women pave the way for the narrative of the virginal conception of Jesus. However, Gaventa offers a further insight into the narrative, and we cite her at some length here:

> The dynamic of threatening and being threatened dominates the entire story of Tamar and Judah, for Tamar's problem arises because Judah (wrongly) understands her to be a threat to the life of his only remaining son. Judah's injustice to her places Tamar in a threatened state, with neither husband nor child, and she seeks rectification through deception which again places her in a threatened state. Rahab poses a threat, not because she is a harlot or because her marriage is irregular, but because her knowledge of Joshua's spies jeopardizes the conquest. When Jericho eventually falls, Rahab in turn becomes the threatened one who must be delivered from the destruction of the remainder of the population. Ruth threatens the status quo by her decision

(in contrast to Orpah's) to stay with Naomi and again by taking the initiative with Boaz. Her actions in both instances become dangerous for herself, since her alliance with Naomi could lead to starvation for them both and her advances to Boaz could lead to the charge of harlotry if he declines to fulfill his obligations as her kinsman. The one action attributed to the "wife of Uriah," the sending of the message of her pregnancy to David, threatens both David and Uriah (whom it eventually destroys); she subsequently becomes the one who lives under the threat of having no father for the child she carries.[18]

Gaventa notes that each of the women "in her own way threatens [the Davidic line] and is in turn threatened."[19] Miriam's pregnancy is in its own way a kind of threat. The pregnancy has come about through the Holy Spirit, but she is threatened with divorce by Joseph, albeit quietly, until the angel instructs him. Then follows the threat from King Herod against "the child and his mother" (Matt 2:11, 14, 20, 21). Gaventa writes, "With his consistent use of the phrase 'the child and his mother' Matthew reflects a powerful connection between the two. When the Magi finally arrived at the place of the star, they see both the child and Mary. The flight to Egypt involves not two parents and the child they protect but Joseph who is instructed to protect 'the child and his mother.' If Jesus is threatened, so is his mother. In Matthew's story, the two belong together."[20] Mary is a woman under threat along with her son.

For the sake of brevity, I am going to assume that Matthew has a copy of St. Mark's Gospel in front of him as he writes, and that he writes according to the scholarly consensus in the mid-80s of the first century. Anyone who wishes to contest this may consult the various points of view that are made available in the various introductions to the Gospels and in the commentaries. In the infancy narrative of Matthew 1—2 the major player is Joseph. Mary is the mother of the child conceived through the Holy Spirit, but it is to Joseph that the angel communicates.

With that in mind it is interesting to see how Matthew alters the text of Mark 3:19-35. In Matthew 12:22-50, we find parallels to everything in this Marcan text with only one exception. When, in Mark 3:19-21, the family says of Jesus, "He has gone out of his mind," Matthew changes this. He simply omits those words, and Raymond Brown provides us with his reason: "Matthew must have understood Mark to refer to the mother and family of Jesus; and Matthew cannot allow that a mother who conceived Jesus through the Holy Spirit could so misunderstand him."[21]

MARY IN THE GOSPEL OF ST. LUKE (LUKE 1:26-38)

"Surely the richest and most influential portrait of Mary in the New Testament is found in the Gospel according to Luke," written probably in the 90s of the first century.[22] New Testament scholar Donald Senior makes the point that the parable of the sower in Luke 8 provides the direction for Lucan insight into Mary. The seed that falls on good ground represents authentic discipleship, and "there is little doubt that this perspective guides Luke's portrayal of Mary."[23] Thus, for example, a woman cries out to Jesus in Luke 11:27-28, "Blessed is the womb that bore you and the breasts that nursed you," to which Jesus replies, "Blessed rather are those who hear the word of God and obey it." Discipleship is the foundation of blessing, and Mary is held up as the model of true discipleship in Luke's infancy narrative.

Images of Mary in the New Testament

Now let us turn to the annunciation scene. Where Joseph was the major player in Matthew, Mary is the major player in Luke's infancy narrative:

> In the sixth month the angel Gabriel was sent by God to a town in Galilee called Nazareth, to a virgin engaged to a man whose name was Joseph, of the house of David. The virgin's name was Mary. And he came to her and said, "Greetings, favored one! The Lord is with you." But she was much perplexed by his words, and pondered what sort of greeting this might be. The angel said to her, "Do not be afraid, Mary, for you have found favor with God. And now, you will conceive in your womb and bear a son, and you will name him Jesus. He will be great, and will be called the Son of the Most High, and the Lord God will give to him the throne of his ancestor David. He will reign over the house of Jacob forever, and of his kingdom there will be no end." Mary said to the angel, "How can this be, since I am a virgin?" The angel said to her: "The Holy Spirit will come upon you, and the power of the Most High will overshadow you; therefore, the child to be born will be holy; he will be called Son of God. And your relative Elizabeth in her old age has also conceived a son; and this is the sixth month for her who was said to be barren. For nothing will be impossible with God." Then Mary said, "Here am I, the servant of the Lord; let it be with me according to your word." Then the angel departed from her. (Luke 1:26–38)

"Of all the New Testament texts about Mary, undoubtedly the most important is the narrative of Luke about the

Annunciation to Mary."[24] This judgment of Ignace de la Potterie is amply verified in the ways in which the annunciation has been the focus of poetic and artistic inspiration and expression, to say nothing of the fact that it is prayed every day as the Angelus.[25] It is clear that the episode speaks of Mary's virginal conception of the Lord Jesus, to be considered in greater detail later. It is equally clear that Mary is the mother of the Messiah, "Son of the Most High" and heir of David, ruling over his house forever. Given the significant facts about Mary it is surely interesting that "Luke identifies Mary with the leanest of descriptions....By stunning contrast with his introductions of Elizabeth and Zechariah, Luke says not a word about Mary's righteousness, her faithfulness to the Law, or her family of origin."[26] Of course, as his Gospel continues, Luke will certainly flesh out his theological portrayal of Mary. Mary's own self-identification in the passage is as the "slave" (*doule*) of the Lord, and as slaves in that context and at that time derived their status from the status of their owner, Mary's status derives "from her obedience to God." "Mary enters the story with virtually no identification beyond her own name, but she leaves identified as a slave of the Lord."[27] She models discipleship.

There are some beautiful insights unearthed in the work of recent feminist theologians, especially the English lay Catholic theologian Tina Beattie. In some very fine meditative passages, Beattie leads us to a deep and challenging appreciation of the annunciation. "Christianity originates in a story of mutual loving endeavor between a woman and God. The Annunciation was not an act of seduction but a free invitation to a woman to participate in God's saving action....God waited while Mary deliberated. The history of the world hung in the balance as a young girl considered the options before her. Then she said, 'I am the handmaid of the Lord, let what you have said be done to me.' And she stepped into the whirlwind."[28] Those words, "God waited while Mary deliberated," are very fine indeed, giving us some small insight into the respect in which God holds his human creatures. This is holy ground, mystery, as an angel conveys the Father's request, the Holy Spirit prepares to overshadow, and the Word is about to be conceived. The mystery comes forcefully to consciousness when we consider the mystery-moment of God's creative-redemptive plan and the subsequent, mystery-moment of Mary's *fiat*, "Let it be with me." Mary's mystery-moment is subsequent because she is free, created such by the God who makes request of her. The story holds together in a magnificently laconic way God's gracious initiative and the uncoerced, human response. There is more, maintains Beattie. In this mystery-moment between God and Mary, patriarchy comes to an end. Beattie gives an interesting twist to this line of thought. "Man has claimed the right to silence every voice but his, but when God speaks to Mary, he restores the power of speech to woman by explicitly excluding man from the event."[29] The voice of the male has been the dominant voice in history, even in the sacred history of Holy Scripture. That voice as the only voice is now stilled. Woman's voice is now heard in a primal and foundational way, and no male is there as Mary says, "Let it be with me."

THE ARK OF THE COVENANT (LUKE 1:39-45, 56)

In those days Mary set out and went with haste to a Judean town in the hill country, where she entered the house of Zechariah and greeted Elizabeth. When Elizabeth heard Mary's greeting, the child leaped in her womb. And Elizabeth was filled with the Holy Spirit and exclaimed with a loud cry, "Blessed are you among women, and blessed is the fruit of your womb. And why has this happened to me, that the mother of my Lord comes to me? For as soon as I heard the sound of your greeting, the child in my womb leaped for joy. And blessed is she who believed that there would be a fulfillment of what was spoken to her by the Lord." ...And Mary remained with her about three months and then returned to her home.

This is the account of the visitation of Mary to Elizabeth. A recent commentator, Australian Archbishop Mark Coleridge, correctly remarks that "attempts to plumb Mary's motivation here are as doomed as they are at other points where the narrator denies the reader any inside view of the characters."[30] The issue is not psychology but theology, but a theology that is difficult to pin down with precision, and both biblical scholars and theologians offer different readings. What is offered here is more of an impressionistic sketch than a comprehensive theological exegesis. First of all, let us note that the text of Luke in 1:35 says that "the Holy Spirit 'overshadows' Mary." The Greek for the word *overshadows* is *episkiazo*. If we turn to the Septuagint version of Exodus 40:35 we read, "Moses was not able to enter the tent of meeting because the cloud settled upon it, and the glory of the LORD filled the tabernacle." "Settled" in this passage is the same verb as in the Lucan passage, *episkiazo*. It seems that St. Luke is casting Mary as the tabernacle of Exodus filled with the very presence of God.[31] To appreciate the meaning of this episode of the visitation in Luke's Gospel, one should then turn to the account of David's dancing before the ark of the covenant in 2 Samuel 6:9-15. The passage opens with a question of David's that recalls the question of Elizabeth, "How can the ark of the LORD come into my care?" (v. 9). Then we are told that the sacred ark containing the tablets of the Law, the word of God, remained in the house of Obed-edom for three months, just as Mary remained in the house of Elizabeth for three months. As the ark was carried into the city of David, we are told that "David danced before the LORD" (v. 14), just as John the Baptist danced *in utero* before the ark/the Lord in Mary's womb. The passage is best understood as a midrashic orchestration, that is, an imaginative and creative theological weaving of biblical text and allusion, of 2 Samuel 6, "likening Mary's journey to the transfer of the Ark of the Covenant and its temporary stay in a welcoming house on the way to Jerusalem."[32] Mary is being represented here as the new ark of the covenant, bearing the very presence of the Word of the Lord.[33]

SINGER OF GOD'S PRAISES (LUKE 1:46-56)

And Mary said,

"My soul magnifies the Lord;
    and my spirit rejoices in God my savior,
for he has looked with favor on the lowliness of his servant;
    Surely, from now on all generations will call me blessed;
for the Mighty One has done great things for me,
    and holy is his name.
His mercy is for those who fear him
    from generation to generation.
He has shown strength with his arm;
    he has scattered the proud in the thought of their hearts.
He has brought down the powerful from their thrones,
    and lifted up the lowly;
he has filled the hungry with good things,
    and sent the rich away empty.

MARY IN THE CHRISTIAN TRADITION

> He has helped his servant Israel,
>   in remembrance of his mercy,
> according to the promise he made to our ancestors,
>   to Abraham and to his descendants forever."

If one looks at the biblical cross references in a modern English translation, the Magnificat turns out to be an anthology of texts, "a cento-like composition, a mosaic of Old Testament expressions drawn from the Septuagint."[34] The texts are not drawn at random from the Old Testament, but rather evince a certain direction. The movement of the Magnificat is from Mary's personal experience of God, "my Savior" (vv. 47–49), to a broad and confident faith in the divine protection, especially to the poor and the marginal of society (vv. 51–53). Lawrence Frizzell, a scholar of the Jewish background of the New Testament, well describes this movement of the Magnificat: "The prayer of Mary moves from the individual experience of God as 'my Savior' to an act of faith in the protection God brings to the poor and oppressed, especially as they acknowledge the vacuum in their lives that can be filled adequately by God alone."[35] This is a key theme of St. Luke so that the Magnificat "serves as a kind of manifesto for the whole gospel."[36] In Luke 1:38, 48, Mary describes herself as the "handmaid" of the Lord, in Greek the *doule* of the Lord. This is the same root word that St. Paul uses of Jesus in the famous hymn of Philippians 2:5–11. There Jesus is described as taking the form of a "slave," in Greek *doulos*. Is this linguistic usage intentional? Does Luke wish to paint Mary as an icon of Jesus, the servant/slave of God? If she is the icon of Jesus the servant, she is also giving utterance in this hymn not only for herself, but also as a representative of God's people, especially the downtrodden and poor.[37] New Testament scholars are quick to point out that "poor" means much more than economically poor. Pulling together references from the Psalms (e.g.,

Pss 18:27; 34:6–7, 18; 35:10; 72:2; 149:4), one might say that as well as being the obviously destitute, the poor are also those who are utterly dependent upon God, those who cry to God out of their need and weakness, and, in that sense, the poor are Israel understood collectively or corporately.[38] Thus this handmaid of the Lord is mightily blessed, but she is also poor, that is, dependent upon God, needy for God.

THE FAITHFUL DISCIPLE (LUKE 8:21; 11:27-28)

> But he said to them, "My mother and my brothers are those who hear the word of God and do it." ... While he was saying this, a woman in the crowd raised her voice and said to him, "Blessed is the womb that bore you and the breasts that nursed you!" But he said, "Blessed rather are those who hear the word of God and obey it."

In both passages from Luke 8:21 and 11:27–28, our Lord defines as his closest relations, his mother and his brothers, those who hear the word of God and obey it. On the surface, it might suggest a certain distance between Jesus and his family, the sort of distance noticed in Mark 3. But there really is no distance here because Mary in the Gospel of St. Luke is par excellence the one who hears the word of God and keeps it. She hears the word of God through Gabriel and conceives that Word in her womb. After finding the child Jesus in the Jerusalem temple, "his mother treasured all these things in her heart" (Luke 2:51). Long before she fed the infant Jesus with her own milk, Mary heard the word of God and kept it. Mary is held up to us by Luke as the model of the faithful disciple.

Finally, let us draw attention to the reappearance of Mary at the beginning of St. Luke's second volume, the Acts of the Apostles. There, in 1:14, we read, "All these (the Twelve) were constantly devoting themselves to prayer, together with certain women, including Mary the mother of Jesus, as well as his brothers." After this she disappears from Acts, and we have no historical knowledge of what happened to her after that.

MARY IN THE GOSPEL OF ST. JOHN

The Gospel of St. John was written most probably between the years 90 and 100. John's Gospel goes beyond the horizon of Matthew and Luke, both of whom describe the birth of Jesus. John, on the other hand, begins with the eternal Word/Logos who takes on flesh in the person of Jesus.

Mary is next found in the episode describing the wedding at Cana in Galilee (2:1–11). In this Gospel it is at Mary's urging that Jesus performs the first of his "signs," the word that John uses for Jesus's miracles. There is a strange conversation between Mary and Jesus. Mary says to him when she discovers that the wine has been used up, "They have no wine" (2:3). Jesus responds, "Woman, what concern is that to you and to me? My hour has not yet come" (2:4). At that point Mary turns to the servants and says, "Do whatever he tells you" (2:5). That is the end of the conversation. It is difficult to know what to make of this very brief conversation, and, moreover, a conversation that has some element of tension about it. "The later tradition would especially recall this incident as evidence of the influence that Mary could have over her son, even when he was not entirely willing: such maternal persuasion was essential to belief in the special powers of Mary's intercessions with her son."[39] These are the words of historian of early Christianity Stephen Shoemaker, and he is surely correct, even though at a theologically reflective level the sentiments are somewhat problematic. Shoemaker goes on to point out that when Jesus leaves Cana for Capernaum, Mary is named as the first of his companions along with his brothers and disciples: "After this he went down to Capernaum with his mother, his brothers, and his disciples" (2:12). From this remark it would seem to be the case that the author of the Gospel thinks of Mary as continuing to be actively involved in the ministry of her son. Arguably, that ministry comes to its fullest and finest expression in our next pericope, John 19:25–27, 30.

However, there may be more to it than that in commenting on those strange words of Jesus: "Woman, what concern is that to you and to me?" (John 2:4). The Greek word used here by the evangelist for "woman" is *gyne*. To help explain this strange address, a number of scripture scholars, for example Brant Pitre, believes that John is modeling the first days of Jesus's ministry in the Gospel on the first week of creation in Genesis. This is how the argument proceeds. In John 1:19, we have the very first day of the Lord's ministry, and this is followed by "the next day" in 1:29. The third day occurs in 1:35 and the fourth day in 1:43, in both cases the text reads "the next day." If we follow with John 2:1, the beginning of the wedding scene at Cana, it reads, "On the third day there was a wedding in Cana of Galilee, and the mother of Jesus was there." Three days more following four prior days makes seven altogether, paralleling the seven days of creation. When Jesus addresses his mother as "woman," he is addressing her as the "woman," in the Septuagint *gyne*, of Genesis 3:15. Joining himself to some insights of the established Johannine scholar Raymond E. Brown, Brant Pitre concludes, "In support of this interpretation, it's important to remember that in the book of Genesis, Eve is called 'Eve' only once; she is called 'woman' *eleven* times. Just as the first Eve invites the first Adam to commit the first sin, so now Mary invites Jesus to perform the first of his 'signs.'"⁴⁰ This way of reading the text finds its final complement when we come to the cross of Jesus in John. There the dying Jesus addresses his mother as "woman" (John 19:26). The evil begun by Eve in Genesis is now overcome on the cross as Jesus establishes the Church.

Mother of the Church (John 19:25-27, 30)

> Meanwhile, standing near the cross of Jesus were his mother, and his mother's sister, Mary the wife of Clopas, and Mary Magdalene. When Jesus saw his mother and the disciple whom he loved standing beside her, he said to his mother, "Woman, here is your son." Then he said to the disciple, "Here is your mother." And from that hour the disciple took her into his own home....When Jesus had received the wine, he said, "It is finished." Then he bowed his head, and he handed over his spirit *(NRSV, except the last sentence which I have translated differently).*

"John 19 customarily serves as the beginning place for identifying Mary as the symbolic mother of the church, as she becomes the mother of the Beloved Disciple."⁴¹ While this is true, it is intriguing that both Mary and the beloved disciple are never actually named in the Gospel of St. John. Both were undoubtedly real, historical persons, but they remain anonymous in St. John for a reason, and that reason is their symbolic function for the author. Jesus gives charge of his mother to the beloved disciple, symbolizing Mary's motherhood of all disciples of Jesus, "Here is your mother." The New Testament scholar Lawrence Frizzell sees in these words an adumbration of the conviction that Jesus was Mary's only child. He writes concerning this verse, "If Mary had other surviving children, all younger than Jesus, one of them should have taken this responsibility."[42] Perhaps this ought not to be pressed too far since this scene, profoundly theological and ecclesiological, may be a Johannine construction. But, if it contains some historical remembrance, Frizzell's remark is suasive. More symbolically, the beloved disciple, like our Lady, stands as the person of faith, an icon of appropriate and committed discipleship. In that sense, "The 'disciple whom Jesus loved' represents all the beloved disciples of Jesus."[43]

Finally, realizing that the end, the *telos*, had come, the *telos* of John 13:1, "Having loved his own who were in the world, he loved them to the end [*eis telos*]," Jesus proclaims, "It is ended [*tetelestai*]," and hands over the Spirit. The Church is animated in the person of his mother and the beloved disciple from the cross as Jesus hands over his Spirit. As Jesus ex-pires, he in-spires the Church. The Church is born from the cross, and as Mary birthed her Son, she is present as his Body, the Church, is given birth on Calvary.

MOTHER OF THE MESSIAH, OF THE CHURCH, OF HOPE (REV 12:1-6)

A great portent appeared in heaven: a woman clothed with the sun, with the moon under her feet, and on her head a crown of twelve stars. She was pregnant and was crying out in birth pangs, in the agony of giving birth. Then another portent appeared in heaven: a great red dragon, with seven heads and ten horns, and seven diadems on his heads. His tail swept down a third of the stars of heaven and threw them to the earth. Then the dragon stood before the woman who was about to bear a child, so that he might devour her child as soon as it was born. And she gave birth to a son, a male child, who is to rule all the nations with a rod of iron. But her child was snatched away and taken to God and to his throne; and the woman fled into the wilderness, where she had a place prepared by God, so that there she can be nourished for one thousand two hundred sixty days.

This is the literary genre of apocalyptic, and in this literary form nothing is what it seems. It operates with symbolism, allusion, and numbers, ultimately to create a climate of confidence in God's final victory over the forces of evil and oppression. Traditionally, in this passage Catholics have seen the figure of Mary, the mother of Jesus and the New Eve. She is so represented in much popular Catholic art. The woman is also interpreted as the heavenly Jerusalem, personified wisdom, or the Church, and perhaps originally as Israel. In this latter interpretation her birth pangs symbolize the eschatological woes that in Judaism and early Christianity are supposed to precede the birth of the Messiah. Ultimately, it is impossible to know with certainty what is the exact meaning of the personification, who is being personified. But is that the most important and compelling aspect of the text? "A woman with child, a woman giving birth. Whatever arguments there may be about how precisely this 'great sign' is to be understood, Christians would agree that Mary belongs with it somewhere. If the sign is not a description of Mary, then Mary is the highest personification of the sign."[44] These are the sentiments of Geoffrey Preston, OP, and they are right on target. He refuses an either-or approach to the text, but reaps a richer harvest, a harvest that sees Mary as the high point of the old Israel and all its aspirations, as *the* woman who gives birth to *the* child, as in that sense the mother of the Church, and a most profound symbol of hope.

CONCLUSION

Our treatment of images of Mary in the New Testament has come to an end. We have turned to different aspects of her person, recognizing the different portraits offered by the evangelists. We have seen her sheer ordinariness in St. Paul and felt her perplexity and probable widowhood in St. Mark. We are no less touched by the annunciation as Mary was touched by Gabriel. Following in St. Luke's rich Marian theology, we are invited to recognize her as the new ark of the covenant, the singer of God's praises and the faithful disciple. In St. John she becomes mother of the Church, and in Revelation she is mother in a number of complementary ways. This tapestry of scriptural Marian images offers all contemporary Christians opportunity to grow in appreciation of God's grace at work in this woman and in ourselves.

3
PATRISTIC MARY

> There was hardly a generation of the early church where a focused interest in Mary of Nazareth cannot be observed, especially if one takes into account the graffiti at the earliest pilgrimage centers, as well as the high theological texts of the patristic theologians.
>
> John A. McGuckin[1]

> To evaluate the extent of Marian influence on the early church is like putting together a jigsaw with many missing pieces.
>
> Tina Beattie[2]

Both John McGuckin, the patristic and Byzantine scholar, and Tina Beattie, the systematic theologian, cited at the opening of this chapter are correct. McGuckin is absolutely on target in suggesting that there never was a time without devotion to Mary, and Beattie is right to point out that in the theological jigsaw puzzle concerning Mary many pieces are unfortunately missing. This may be due in part to the omnipresence of maternal deities in paganism. Such maternal-fertility deities were everywhere to be found throughout the Mediterranean region and the Middle East where Christianity was to take root. Christians naturally would want to distance their faith and their growing Marian devotion from this popular pagan phenomenon. Given this complex perspective, the question before us is, "How to begin?"

Let's cluster how Christians thought about Mary in the working out of God's redemptive plan in the patristic period around the following headings:[3]

- Mary as the New Eve
- the virginity of Mary
- Mary as Mother of God
- the holiness of Mary
- the dormition of Mary, or her assumption into heaven after her death

As we move through these issues, we shall see that they necessarily shade into one another, and never stand in isolation. They interweave, one might say flawlessly, providing us with a fine Marian patristic tapestry, and a tapestry rooted in the "sense of the faithful" as devotion to Mary gained momentum in the Church.

MARY AS THE NEW EVE

"The primordial patristic insight with respect to the Mother of Christ is the vision of Mary as the New Eve,"[4] and as Kallistos Ware, the Orthodox theologian and hierarch, felicitously puts it, "Eve chose freely when she fell, and in the same way Mary chose freely when she obeyed."[5] To flesh out this insight let us turn first of all to Justin of Rome who seems to have been among the first to make this connection. Justin contrasts the disobedience of Eve with the obedience of Mary, the one leading to the fall, the other leading to Redemption.[6] Essentially Justin, writing in a Roman Christian community troubled by Valentinian Gnosticism and Marcionite rejection of the Old Testament, is making the point that the pattern of redemption parallels the pattern of the fall. Both came about through the agency of a virgin, the fall through Eve and the redemption through Mary. Justin does not speculate about Mary. His real interest is Christology and, in that sense, Mary serves Christology. Here we may see a major foundation of patristic thinking about our Lady.

Next comes the great bishop of Lyons, Irenaeus. Irenaeus took hold of the analogy provided by Justin, the Eve-Mary connection, and developed it. Walter Burghardt, the twentieth-century Jesuit patristic scholar and well-known homilist, provides a superb summary of the theological principles that ground Irenaeus's understanding of Mary. "There is the principle termed *recapitulatio*: the human dilemma, the paradoxical imperative that fallen nature must be lifted to God by the nature that had fallen, is resolved in the Word made flesh, who identifies himself with humanity by becoming its second head (*caput*). And there is the complementary principle called *recirculatio*: the process of restoration is fated to correspond inversely to that of the fall, somewhat as a knot is untied—a complicated knot, fashioned of Eve's disobedience as well as the rebellion of Adam."[7] Eve's disobedience and refusal to believe are contrasted with Mary's obedience and belief. Through Eve came death, through Mary life and salvation. There is an inversion from the fall to redemption, and central to this process is Mary, mother of the Redeemer.[8]

The Eve-Mary parallelism has remained a favorite theme in Christian preaching and devotional literature as Christians searched the Scriptures seeking further to understand the mysterious pattern of redemption, and as Walter Burghardt notes, it continued to be very popular: "From the death of

John of Damascus in the middle of the eighth century the witnesses to the Eve-Mary parallelism follow one another in an endless wave, across the whole of the Latin Middle Ages, down to our own time."[9]

THE VIRGINITY OF MARY

Following upon the conviction of Christ's virginal conception in the Gospels of Matthew and Luke, the tradition continues to accept this conviction and to develop it. Getting immediately into the second century, we find Ignatius of Antioch (ca. 35–107) for whom "the virgin birth is a piece of the church's recognized tradition, to which he refers in fixed phrases reminiscent of confessional formulae."[10] In other words, the ways in which Ignatius speaks of the virginal conception of Jesus suggest that even as early as his time at the beginning of the second century of Christianity that conviction may have become part of a very early Christian creed, perhaps in preparation for the sacrament of baptism. While there can be no doubt about Ignatius's belief in the virginal conception of Jesus, at the same time, the central emphasis for him is on the real incarnation of the Word of God, an emphasis that he insists upon in opposition to those who hold a docetic Christology, that is to say, a Christology that downplays or repudiates the genuine humanity of Christ. It was ever a challenge for Christians to hold together both the divinity of Christ and his humanity, the temptation being constantly to downplay the one or the other.

Moving on to Justin in second-century Rome, we find him referring to the virginal conception on a number of occasions.[11] Justin believes the virginal conception of Jesus to be a well-established element in the Christian tradition. At the same time, he is aware of Christians who think that Jesus is the son of both Joseph and Mary, but he reproaches them as missing something important in the Christian proclamation.[12] Interestingly enough, as Justin attempts to defend the truth of the virginal conception against mythical pagan thought, he points to what might be described as mythically distorted anticipations of the virginal conception, in which "heroes and extraordinary personalities…are descended from Zeus."[13] Although not fully developed, Justin considers that some pagan ideas about the gods/divine heroes are shadowy anticipations of the Christian revelation. Irenaeus developed a fully incarnational theology, and in that context, the virginal conception of Jesus is important for him. From Mary comes Jesus's humanity and his kinship with David; from his origin from the Holy Spirit comes his being Son of God.[14]

The virginal conception of Jesus then in the early Christian centuries was virtually unquestioned because of its presence and affirmation in the infancy narratives of the Gospels of Matthew and Luke and its possible inclusion in some early developing Christian creed. A quite different question has to do with the "brothers of Jesus" as found in the Scriptures. How are these brothers to be understood? Are they the children of Mary and Joseph? Gradually, the Christian community worked its way toward the affirmation of Mary's perpetual virginity. Among the majority of Roman Catholics and the Orthodox churches, this conviction has remained constant and the belief in Mary's perpetual virginity continued to grow and the definitive pronouncement about Mary's perpetual virginity came at the Lateran Council in 649.

MARY, MOTHER OF GOD

"This one word, Mother of God/*Theotokos* provides the key to the whole Orthodox understanding of Mary."[15] Development in Marian theology between the Council of Nicaea

Patristic Mary

(325) and the Council of Ephesus (431) was greatly influenced by the growing prestige throughout the Church of virginity, both East and West. After the Edict of Milan (313), the persecution of the Church came to an end. Toleration was the order of the day, and the age of the martyrs was over. The fervor that found expression in martyrdom now found its expression in asceticism and in the life of consecrated virginity. So much is this the case that Mary has been described in this period as "the archetypal hesychast (reflective mystic), and mother of all virgin ascetics."[16]

The Council of Ephesus in 431 maintained that the title for Mary, *Theotokos*/Mother of God was entirely appropriate. This was to counter the theology of Nestorius, Patriarch of Constantinople (428–31). He became patriarch in 428, the personal choice of Emperor Theodosius II (408–50). On one occasion, a well-known preacher named Proclus, who was himself to become Patriarch of Constantinople in 434, preached a sermon honoring the Blessed Virgin Mary. He praised her in the traditional ways that patristic authors had done. However, he also in the course of his sermon called Mary "the holy *Theotokos* Mary."[17] At this point during his sermon Patriarch Nestorius took over and made a correction of Proclus. Nestorius insisted that Mary was indeed worthy of all praise, but she could not be called *Theotokos*. For Nestorius, because it was only the human nature of Christ that was born of the Virgin Mary, Mary should not be called *Theotokos*/Mother of God. For him that seemed to imply that she had given birth to God, to the divine nature itself. So, he suggested that instead of this title she should be called *Christotokos*/"the one who gave birth to Christ." Nestorius's suggestion offended not only the fast-growing Marian piety of believers but also theologians. At a synod in Rome in 430, Pope Celestine (d. 432) condemned Nestorius. The Emperor Theodosius called a council of the church at Ephesus so that Nestorius could answer the charges against him. Nestorius was deposed as Patriarch of Constantinople, excommunicated, and the Council of Ephesus in 431 made it official that Mary is to be known as *Theotokos*/Mother of God. "If anyone does not confess that Emmanuel is God in truth, and therefore that the holy Virgin is the Mother of God [*Theotokos*] (for she bore in a fleshly way the Word of God become flesh), let him be anathema."[18] With Nestorius deposed, Proclus became Patriarch of Constantinople. From here on out Mary was universally acclaimed as *Theotokos*, Mother of God. After the Council of Ephesus in the East, the title for Mary of *Theotokos*/Mother of God now became widely used. In a similar way, the allied title of Mary as *aeiparthenos*/ever-Virgin, also became much more widespread.

The councils of Ephesus and Chalcedon in the fifth century, along with all the christological debates involved, gave further impetus to Mariology. The reason is obvious: if Jesus is truly consubstantial with the Father, and so is divine, and if Mary is his mother, there must be a fundamental sense in which she is truly Mother of God, *Theotokos*. In that precise sense, Mariology is a function of Christology. Yet it was inevitable that her status would be more developed among the faithful, that devotion to her would grow, and that churches would be dedicated to her.

THE HOLINESS OF MARY

Though perhaps not in so many words and not so often in explicit terms, patristic authors in the first three centuries clearly considered Mary to be holy, to be especially privileged by God. Their concern has more to do with the development of Christology and so with the sinlessness of Christ. The all-holiness of Mary as an important Christian conviction in the West comes to a head with St. Augustine (354–430) and the

Patristic Mary

Pelagians. Pelagius (ca. 354–418) believed that human beings had a native ability to live lives of goodness and morality, and so he denied what came to be known as original sin. To demonstrate his conviction, he provides a list of individuals who have lived holy, moral lives. "The names range from Abel through Abraham to Joseph and John, from Deborah to Elizabeth,' and in fact the Mother of our Lord and Savior too, whom piety must needs confess free from sin.' Ambrose had found no imperfection in Mary; Pelagius asserted on principle that sin *could* be found."[19] Augustine replies to him positively—that is to say, only Mary is free from sin, but he insists that her sinless state is an expression of the triumph of grace, not of nature. It is the work of God in her, and not her own autonomous doing.[20] While the intricacies of the theological debate continued for centuries, much popular sentiment advocated the position that from her very beginning Mary was sinless. This popular sentiment continued throughout the tradition, albeit not without controversy, until in Catholic terms it was settled by Pope Pius IX's 1854 dogmatic declaration of the immaculate conception of Mary. The dogma of the immaculate conception is not something normally accepted by Orthodox Christians, despite their clear affirmations of Mary's holiness and freedom from actual sin. The Orthodox theologian Kallistos Ware, himself a well-established patristic scholar, makes the Orthodox case in a particularly persuasive way. This is what he writes:

> Orthodox feel that the Latin doctrine of the Immaculate Conception separates Mary from the rest of the descendants of Adam, putting her in a different class from all the other righteous men and women of the Old Testament, and in this way destroying the continuity of sacred history....The Latin theory of the Immaculate Conception, so it seems to

Orthodoxy, weakens this precious link between the Virgin and the remainder of humanity before Christ.[21]

Ultimately, there is no serious dispute on the issue between the Orthodox and Roman Catholics. What we find in both of them is clear devotion to and reflection upon the holiness of Mary. What is especially valuable in the way Ware expresses himself is the clear connection between Mary and the Church, the Church of the Old Testament as well as the Church of the New Testament. "What is here in question...is a difference, not in the Roman Catholic and Orthodox attitudes towards Mary, but in our respective doctrines of original sin."[22]

MARY'S DORMITION OR ASSUMPTION INTO HEAVEN

"The early church is silent on the destiny of Mary, in the sense that no extant document deals explicitly with that destiny until a half-century after Nicaea....Even when popular faith has been quickened, there is little evidence in the West of a theological movement to rival the homiletic productions of the East....Briefly, between Nicaea and Ephesus the allusions to Mary's destiny are rare and insignificant."[23] The first witness to the assumption into heaven of Mary in Western theological literature is an apocryphal Gospel, the *Transitus Beatae Mariae* of Pseudo-Melito, probably to be dated about the middle of the sixth century (*Transitus*, 15.2ff.). The text stresses the parallelism that should be there between Christ and Mary in terms of victory over death. The text talks about the death and burial of Mary and the reunion of her soul and body without any delay, and thus her assumption into heaven. Walter Burghardt comments on the importance of the text that "it witnesses indisputably to the feeling of the faithful for Mary, a growing awareness of her dignity."[24] This feeling of the faithful for Mary was to remain a permanent feature of the Christian tradition, and often came up against the views of the academic theological community.

AT THE CLOSE OF THE PATRISTIC AGE: JOHN OF DAMASCUS (CA. 675-749)

Very little is known in detail of John's life. John of Damascus was the grandson of the last Byzantine governor of Damascus, a Syrian Arab Christian named Mansour ibn Sargun, and the son of a senior figure in the financial administration of the new Muslim state, Sergios ibn Mansour. The Arabic name he would have used early in life was Yanah ibn Mansur ibn Sargun. He grew up as a close companion of the future Caliph al-Yazid. "The two youths' drinking bouts in the streets of Damascus were the subject of much horrified gossip in the new Islamic capital."[25] Eventually, John assumed his father's position in the Muslim administration and throughout his life he remained a favorite of the caliph, although after the latter's death he was falsely accused of collusion with the Byzantine Emperor. The first part of his life was lived in Damascus, the city of his birth, and then later in Palestine, very probably Jerusalem, where he became a monk.

John was known in Constantinople as *Sarakenophron*, "Saracen-minded." In many ways he is a bridge between Christianity and Islam and in fact wrote the first informed treatise on Islam by a Christian. He seems to have regarded Islam as a Judeo-Christian sect. He retired to the monastery of Mar Saba and devoted his declining years to writing homilies and to refuting heresies. His major work is known as *The Fount of*

Knowledge, which was probably the most sophisticated and encyclopedic theological work before St. Thomas Aquinas. Actually, Aquinas drew on John's theology, and it is said that he read a few pages of John's book every day of his life. William Dalrymple writes of John's view of Islam: "It never seems to have occurred to John that Islam might be a separate religion, and although he looked down at it with considerable suspicion, he nevertheless applauds the way Islam converted the Arabs from idolatry, and writes with admiration of its single-minded emphasis on the unity of God."[26] John's theology has been described by one of his best contemporary commentators, Andrew Louth, in the following way:

> John is a representative of a determining period in the development of the Byzantine theological tradition, rather than an original thinker. This is more than a simple consequence of the horror with which the Byzantine world greeted any kind of innovation. Anything new tended to be disguised as tradition. John developed a tradition of learning that knew where to look in the Fathers for answers to all theological questions, and he responded to these questions by reproducing the best that he could find. He had, one might say, a genius for selection; but even this was probably not simply a matter of his personal giftedness as a learned scholar: he belonged to a tradition that had been sifting the works of the Fathers for generations.[27]

John's respect for the tradition he has received goes far beyond what we might think of as mere repetition. Yes, he hands on what he has received but sparkling with the rhetoric that reflects his own appropriation of that tradition but "the structure of

Patristic Mary

his synthesis, as well as many of its details, testify to his own theological insight and ability."[28]

John wrote three homilies on the dormition of Mary. The distinguished Jesuit patristic scholar Brian E. Daley describes them in the following words: "The most celebrated of all the ancient homilies for the feast of the Dormition, however, are those forming the trilogy for the feast composed by St. John of Damascus."[29] These three homilies were delivered, sometime in the 730s or 740s, as a trio and as part of an all-night vigil. The first homily is taken up with the incarnation, the second with the dormition and the assumption of Mary into heaven, and the third is a celebration of that assumption.[30] It is very likely that the three homilies were delivered in the church near Gethsemane, which was the traditional location of Mary's tomb. What is preeminently clear from John's three homilies is the conviction, the widespread conviction and not simply his own, that it was entirely fitting that our Lady should be taken up into heaven at her death, bringing to completion the work of redemption begun in and with her.[31]

In the second homily we find John recognizing as did so many that Mary suffered none of the pains of childbirth. However, he goes on to say that she suffered the pains of Calvary.[32] When we move to the third homily, the shortest of the three, we find it to be largely a litany of praise of the Mother of God. Within this beautiful litany we find that the assumption of our Lady is grounded in the incarnation of the Eternal Word in her and brought to completion as an appropriate work of grace.[33]

CONCLUSION

From Ignatius of Antioch all the way through the patristic tradition until John of Damascus we have found Mary, the mother of Jesus, celebrated and praised. From the images of Mary in the New Testament, rereading the Old Testament in a typological fashion and harnessing Mariology to Christology among the fathers of the Church—all these texts and the authors and communities behind them witness to a love for Mary and devotion to her, and most especially among the ordinary faithful. This love and devotion were to continue throughout the entirety of the Christian religion, and also to find root in Islam, and so, after a brief excursus into the Syriac Christian world, it will be to the Muslim Mary that we direct our attention.

4

SYRIAC MARY

> Wherever the Fathers unfold their theology with its veils of imagery, we discover a wealth of symbols and of truths clothed in symbols, which could give new life through our modern dogmatic expressions, perhaps still all too much dominated as they are by apologetics and canon law.
>
> Hugo Rahner, SJ[1]

So far, we have been considering Mary in terms of Greek and Latin authors. Now we shall turn briefly to Syriac authors. Syriac is a dialect of Aramaic, the language of Jesus. It became the language of the Christian communities of what would be today Iraq and Iran, in early Christian times the easternmost parts of the Roman Empire. Most of the texts written in Syriac are Christian, but while some may go back perhaps to the second century, "The golden age of Syriac literature may be said to extend from the fourth to the sixth century."[2] Writing almost half a century ago, the great English Jesuit patristic scholar and Syriacist Fr. Robert Murray (1925–2018) penned these words: "In 1974 it was hardly an exaggeration to say that theological study of the early Syriac fathers was still in its infancy. Critical editions of many major Syriac writers were still comparatively few."[3] Thankfully much has changed since 1974 and editions of Syriac texts of the fathers and studies of Syriac theology have flourished in more recent decades.

When it comes to exegesis, Syriac theologians use typology. Typology does not often sit well with more contemporary approaches to scriptural interpretation. However, the outstanding Christian Syriac scholar Sebastian Brock offers a good description of typology and makes a brief but persuasive defense of it: "[Typology seeks to make] connections between persons, objects and events...either as complementing, or as contrasting, each other," and typological exegesis may "make meaningful, and give insight into, some aspects of a mystery that cannot be fully explained."[4] Brock goes on to offer some other fine ideas about typology in modern theology:

> Indeed, one wonders whether this approach does not offer the openings of a *via tertia* (third way) for twentieth-century Western Christianity in its dilemma when faced with the liberal critical approach to the Bible that to many seems purely destructive, on the one side, and a distastefully fundamentalist approach on the other. It must of course be realized that typological exegesis can never, by its very nature, lay any claims to scientific objectivity, seeing that it belongs to a completely different mode of thought.[5]

Brock's words are helpful for the Christian community that wants to avoid, on the one hand, what might seem like the overly skeptical conclusions of the historical-critical methods of interpreting Scripture and, on the other hand, the literalism of fundamentalism.

Syriac Mary

With Brock's considerations in mind, let us turn to the Syriac text known as the *Odes of Solomon*. This work, going back perhaps to the late first or early second century, contains forty-two short hymns. Ode 19 speaks of Mary.[6] In this hymn the Son is the cup milked from the Father, a clear affirmation of the consubstantiality of the Son with the Father, centuries before the Council of Nicaea (325). The Holy Spirit interestingly is the one who milked the Father, "she who milked him," and while the image may seem a little strange to modern ears, it is a fully orthodox expression of trinitarian doctrine. Mary is the one who received this trinitarian cup in conceiving the Son. The text with these homely metaphors tells us that Mary is part of the divine plan of salvation. She received the "cup" that is the Son, who himself came from the milk of the Father, the Holy Spirit being the milkmaid, so to speak. The image of the Trinity in the first three lines is very beautiful, even if for some it might jar because the Father being milked may seem to be feminine and the Spirit is described as "she." Syriac theological authors work more with imagery and metaphors than with abstract philosophical ideas, and so they simply would not be troubled with philosophical-theological objections to the ways in which they express the mysteries of faith.

EPHREM OF NISIBIS

Moving later into the Syriac tradition we find the great father of the Church Deacon Ephrem of Nisibis (ca. 306–73). "The Syriac image of Mary finds its most powerful expression in the commentaries and hymns of Ephrem the Syrian."[7] Indeed, Ephrem has been called by Fr. Robert Murray "the greatest poet of the patristic age, and perhaps the only theologian-poet to rank beside Dante."[8] Ephrem is fond of writing about the womb of Mary containing paradoxically the uncontainable God, as in his *Hymns on the Nativity* 21:6–8. There we find Ephrem contrasting the "vast wombs of all creation," which have come to be through the Word/Son and which, therefore, are somehow expressive of his very being with the small womb of Mary through which he became flesh.[9] The greatness and transcendence of God is extolled, and simultaneously his immanent presence in creation is expressed, "in the vast wombs of all creation." We get a sense here of the cosmic presence of the divine throughout creation. Paradoxically, then, the Word through whom all creation came into being, is "contained" in the womb of Mary. Ephrem loves paradox and through the paradoxes of this hymn, not only do we find affirmed the greatness of God but also Mary's divine maternity.

The Eve-Mary typology noticed in other fathers East and West is often found in Ephrem, especially in his "Hymns on the Nativity."[10] "The robe of glory" is an interesting motif found in Syriac theology. Adam and Eve lost their "robes of glory" when they were exiled from the Garden of Eden. The incarnation of the Word of God restored the "robe of glory," and here too the mother of Jesus plays a role. In "the Hymns on the Nativity" XVI.11 we read that while the Word/Son put on the robe of humankind in Mary, she "put on his glory." The language of this hymn reminds me of a medallion found high in a window of the Basilica of St. Mary Major in Rome. In this beautiful medallion Mary is portrayed as an old lady sitting on her Risen Son's lap as she is about to be received in glory. Fire is another image often used of Christ by Ephrem as in "Hymns on the Faith," X.17, where we find that Fire and Spirit, the transforming Spirit of God is the agent of the incarnation in the virginal conception in Mary's womb, and it is the same transforming agent in the sacrament of baptism, *and* it is the same transforming agent of bread and wine in the Eucharist.

Like virtually all patristic writers, the Syriac Ephrem emphasizes the virginity of Mary both before the birth of

Christ and at the time of his birth. Our Lady for Ephrem could not have experienced the pain of childbirth because she was exempt by grace from the curse of Adam and Eve's fall.[11] Ephrem obviously endorses the growing and widespread view of the perpetual virginity of Mary. He also, in terms of what he says about the pain of childbirth, seems to be aware of the second-century text the *Protoevangelium of James* in which this idea first seems to come to expression, and so he accepts that Mary is free from the travail of childbirth.

JACOB OF SERUGH

Jacob of Serugh (451–521) is yet another important Syriac theologian, often regarded as second only in stature to Ephrem. Jacob composed a number of homilies on the Virgin Mary. Mary's pure and clean soul reversed the defeat brought about by Eve, initiating the "Life, Light and victory" of the incarnation-redemption.[12] Along with other Syriac theologians Jacob acknowledges the perpetual virginity of the Virgin Mary "but regard[s] it as a mystery which should not be pried into."[13] This apophatic note is one he shares with Ephrem: God and the things of God are the deepest mysteries and do not yield themselves to rational analysis.

A really interesting example of Jacob's typology may be found here. For Jacob, Adam begot Eve as the Holy Spirit blew upon his face, that is to say, without intercourse. Mary received this same Spirit too, and she gave birth to a Son. While Adam gave birth to Eve, the "mother of all living things" without intercourse, through the action of the Spirit, so Mary, without human agency, gave birth to the Lord Jesus, "the fountain of all life."[14] Here we see a certain play in Jacob's typology. Jacob sees Mary corresponding to Adam in her miraculous conception. As Adam miraculously "conceives" Eve through the breath of the Holy Spirit, so Mary miraculously conceives Jesus through the same Holy Spirit. At the same time, just as Eve becomes the mother of all living, so Mary becomes the mother of the new humankind, in Christ.

CONCLUSION

Dipping into the Syriac tradition for thinking about our Blessed Lady, albeit all too briefly here, seems to me valuable for various reasons. First, it enables us to recognize what we might call the universal attraction of Mary and devotion to her among the Christians of these early centuries. Second, while both Greek and Latin Marian reflection, as it develops, moves within the orbit of somewhat abstract Hellenistic philosophical vocabulary, the Syriac fathers seem much more at ease with image and metaphor. There is a place for both approaches, of course, but the Syriac tradition, as it becomes better known, may have a greater popular appeal, as suggested by the words of Hugo Rahner in the quotation from him that opens this chapter.

5

CELTIC MARY

Clearly Patrick was a great man of prayer, and his prayer was nourished on biblical imagery and biblical language….There is nothing whatever artificial or forced or extravagant about it. His piety is warm, deep, living, and never insincere.

Richard P. C. Hanson[1]

The world of Celtic Christian theology has had a renewed interest in academic as well as more popular theology and spirituality, but little or no attention has been paid to what it has to say about our Blessed Lady Mary.

ST. PATRICK (CA. 385–461)

The opening words of this chapter from theologian, patristic scholar, and authority on St. Patrick, Richard Hanson, could not be more accurate. He summarizes superbly what we know for certain about the saint. Patrick was a Christian bishop from somewhere in Britain, the embattled edge of a then crumbling Roman Empire. Thomas O'Loughlin, a specialist in

Celtic Christianity, history and theology is led to say, "Patrick is probably the best known fifth-century Christian in the world today. Theologians may argue that Augustine (354–430) was, and perhaps still is, more influential for how Christians present their beliefs, but how many New Yorkers parade on 28 August (his feast day)?"[2]

There are two texts that are from a scholarly perspective safely ascribed to Patrick, the *Confession* and the *Letter to the Soldiers of Coroticus*, the *Letter* probably written first. In fact, these are the only two documents that can be claimed to come from the Church in Britain/Ireland in the fifth century. That makes them doubly precious. They are compared with the works of other patristic authors who were his contemporaries and warmly described by Thomas O'Loughlin as follows:

> While the sermons of Caesarius of Arles [ca. 468/470–542] and the wise instructions of Eucherius of Lyons [ca. 380–449] bring us face-to-face with profound Christian learning, Patrick's works bring us a living human being. We read Patrick's two surviving documents and feel we are coming into contact with a real man of flesh and blood. We sense that he puts himself into his writings; we sense his hurts, angers, hopes, and fears.[3]

This is not the place to provide an account of Patrick's texts, but what we can say by way of summary is that he comes across as a real human being, as a very ordinary man, one who faced many challenges in life, and one who achieved a remarkable degree of self-knowledge. While he may not have been the first to bring Christianity to Celtic Ireland, he is certainly the one who put his stamp on the Celtic Christian church that came after him.[4] Furthermore, I think we can recognize a strong experiential component to the Christian faith of the

Celtic Mary

Celts, what we might call "Christian ordinariness," perhaps to be contrasted with the more speculative theological component of the great patristic writers of the Mediterranean basin and the Syriac East.

A Word on Mary from the *Stowe Missal*.[5]

A missal is the book of prayers used for the celebration of the Eucharist. The *Stowe Missal* is the oldest surviving missal from the early Irish church. It was probably produced around the year 800 in a Celtic monastery in Tallaght, Co. Dublin.[6] At this time, missals used for the celebration of Mass were marked by a certain amount of variety reflecting the customs and traditions of the locality in which they were produced and used. It was not until the liturgical reforms resulting from the sixteenth-century Council of Trent that greater liturgical uniformity became a standard characteristic of missals. As Thomas O'Loughlin has said, "In the earlier period missals had no definite shape as books and their form depended on the particular conditions of when and where they were commissioned and the availability of resources."[7] In the *Stowe Missal* the celebration of the Eucharist began with a penitential litany, not unlike the beginning of Mass today. After the invocation of Christ, the saints are named, including, among others, Sts. Peter, Paul, Andrew, James, Mark, and Luke. The list of saints is a mix of apostles and Gospel writers, and "in all likelihood was intended as a recollection of the gathering of the apostles at the Last Supper...and so they are the company to which the congregation at the Eucharist aspires to belong."[8] However, in this list, Mary is named first after Christ. Of course, we do not know if historically our Lady was present at the Last Supper, but what is interesting is that this Irish community of Christians cannot think of celebrating the Eucharist without her presence, along with the other saints named Mary in their midst.

MARY IN THE CHRISTIAN TRADITION

RETRIEVING THE CELTIC CHRISTIAN TRADITION

The well-known spiritual author Esther de Waal has done a great service for Christians in selecting and editing a fine anthology of Celtic hymns and songs from the famous collection *Carmina Gadelica* by Alexander Carmichael (1832–1912).[9] For sixty years Carmichael traveled around the Scottish Highlands and Islands collecting the folklore of the Gaelic-speaking people, a culture that is now all but lost and forgotten. This was a culture steeped in Christian tradition, in poetry, prayer, and song.

> [These Gaelic speaking Christians] gave him the prayers whose daily and yearly rhythms marked their lives: prayers from birth to death, from dawn to dusk, from the start of the year until its close, for they lived quite naturally in a state of prayer. It was a praying which responded to, and grew out of, their way of life, not one imposed from outside it by an institutional church, even though most of them were Roman Catholics. Carmichael noted in passing, however, that although these prayers had been rescued chiefly from among the Roman Catholics and in the islands, they were equally common among Protestants and on the mainland.[10]

Carmichael thought that these ancient hymns and prayers might go back to the monasteries of Derry in the north of Ireland or the island of Iona. Modern scholars tell us this is unlikely. But however unlikely it is that the textual roots are to be found in monastic communities, the roots are certainly to be found in the earliest Christian traditions of these Celtic peoples of Ireland and Scotland. That seems both sensible and certain.

THE CELTIC MARY

Esther de Waal beautifully describes the spiritual horizon of these people: "[The hymns and prayers] grew out of their sense of the presence of God as the most immediate reality in their lives. Religion permeated everything they did.... They found it natural to assume that God was lovingly concerned in everything they did. They felt totally at home with God....There is no divide here between this world and the next. Heaven and earth are interconnected and interacting."[11]

Those whose names are familiar from the litany of the saints feature in these hymns and prayers, not so much as mighty heavenly potentates, but rather as humans-in-heaven who are kin to us. "St. Peter is not the man with the keys but the man of 'sleep and of fear.' But, above all, Mary, while still hailed as the Queen of Heaven, is also a woman to whom to confide about duties around the house, a woman who knew their sort of life since she herself had experienced simplicity, hardship and tears."[12]

In one of these Celtic hymns the Virgin Mary is described as "most glorious" with angels bowing before her and the Christ child, and with the consent of God the Father (the King of life), Mary is raised up, she is honored, she is no ordinary woman. Then the tone changes. Petitions are asked of her, not in her own right, as it were, but because she is "Mother of wondrous power," that is to say in more familiar terms Mother of God, the great *Theotokos* of the Council of Ephesus in 431. The petitions are particularly interesting. She is asked to "bless the provision...the board...the ear, the corn, the food." These are the necessities of life. It is as if she as a woman, looking after her family and feeding them knows experientially how important it is to make sure that food is available. In this fashion, she is an ordinary woman with ordinary women. One of the features that strikes me as particularly interesting is a phrase in these hymns: "Christ so young on her breast." This phrase seems something of a common motif in these Celtic hymns and prayers. Why, however, the words "so young on her breast"? Perhaps it has something to do with the high rate of infant mortality in ancient times, so that the child "so young on her breast" becomes a powerful symbol of Mary's co-vulnerability with women in this condition.

Mary's maternity finds emphasis in these Celtic prayers, and the one who prays is confident in Mary's everlasting care as a mother. The images are all so very ordinary. In one of his last theological essays, the Scottish systematic theologian John Macquarrie, himself strongly identified as a Christian Celt, speaks in the same ordinary vein of Celtic Mary.[13] This may have at least in part been due to his son, Alan Macquarrie, a distinguished ecclesiastical historian specializing in early Scottish church history.[14] Though Macquarrie's interest in Celtic spirituality and theology undoubtedly goes back a long way, it seems to be his son's interest and research that has further sparked the father's. John Macquarrie finds in Celtic theology an anticipation of his own version of God's immanence, God's real presence found within his creation. In reality, Macquarrie would see his theology of God and of God's presence on a continuum with his Celtic forebears. Thus, describing Celtic religious thought, Macquarrie says, "God was conceived not so much as a distant power in the heavens as a circumambient and inescapable presence here on earth."[15] This circumambient and inescapable presence of God did not stand in contestation with God's transcendence. Rather, this fundamental conviction invited "a tremendous sense of intimacy with God," and an intimacy that found expression in poetry and daily prayers. For example, a prayer for lying down to sleep at night acknowledges God, the holy Trinity, laying down alongside the sleeper, as it were, keeping the sleeper within the loving embrace of God. It is a full-blown trinitarian prayer—Father, Son, and Holy Spirit are each addressed—but with a very powerful sense of the immediate presence of the triune God to the sleeper.[16]

This closeness to and intimacy with God extended also to the angels, the saints, and especially to our Blessed Lady. The Celts had a very strong corporate sense of church. The Communion of Saints was a daily experiential reality for them. In the vernacular Gaelic poetry and prayers, Mary becomes a daily experiential reality as we have recognized, in line with the immanence of God. This is how Macquarrie expresses it: "Mary does not appear as she does in a church, in a statue, let us say, or in a stained-glass window. She is one of the community, sharing the home and the work-place....So Mary is in the kitchen, at the bedside of the sick, among the farm animals, comforting the dying....The Celt spoke of her with an affectionate intimacy."[17] As with the holy Trinity, there is no dumbing down in Celtic theology and spirituality of our Blessed Lady as *Theotokos*, Mother of God. At the same time, the Celtic instinct is to see Mary as very close to them in the sheer ordinariness of life. She is not remote, and her maternal embrace is experienced in the midst of the daily events.

CONCLUSION

From at least the time of St. Patrick, contemporary of St. Augustine of Hippo in the fifth century, Christianity took root in Celtic lands and cultures and began to flourish. While some of the texts referred to in this chapter cannot be taken as very early Christian texts, the sentiments that they exemplify certainly can. Along with the rest of the Christian world the Celts demonstrate devotion to Mary, but a devotion that recognizes her not only in her exalted status as Mother of God but especially also as one of themselves. Their way of thinking about our Blessed Lady is ordinary, woven from the tapestry of their daily domestic lives, and very experiential—just like what we know of St. Patrick's own theology.

6
MUSLIM MARY

> The Muslim Mary is not primarily celebrated as mother of Christ, but as a distinctive archetype of female prayerfulness and patience in adversity. As such she is "a sign for the worlds."
>
> Timothy Winter[1]

> The average Christian's knowledge of Islam is still woefully weak. In many cases it is grotesquely distorted because of age-old prejudices and misconceptions.
>
> R. J. McCarthy[2]

In earlier chapters we have seen the growth of devotion to Mary and reflection about her throughout the territories controlled by the Roman Empire. To that growth we must add a comment from social historian Miri Rubin who writes, "While in the Christian Empire Mary was being thanked and praised, painted and sung with the support and approval of the imperial family, monks and lay people, her figure was being re-evaluated within the sensibility of early Islam."[3] Islam was about to shake the world, especially the established Christian world, and in this shaking this religious faith had a place not only for Isa, the Muslim name for Jesus, but also for his mother, Maryam.

In his recent Paulist Press book on Mary, Fr. Thomas Casey opens his chapter "Mary and Islam" with these words:

> Catholics and, indeed, all Christians are usually surprised to discover how positively the Virgin Mary is depicted in the Qur'an. She is the only woman mentioned by name in this book that is so sacred to Muslims. Other women in the Qur'an are known as "the wife of Adam" or "Pharaoh's wife," and so on, but not by their own names. Mary is the exception. She is mentioned by name over thirty times: that's more often than her name appears in the New Testament.[4]

What a great way to introduce our chapter!

The prophet Muhammad (ca. 570–629) is the founder of Islam, which literally means "submission to the will of God." Muslim doctrine is laid down in the Qur'an and in the Sunna, that is, the "customs" of the Prophet and of his immediate followers. If one scrolls carefully through these two foundations of Islam, one finds among other things elements of Judaism and Christianity, not surprisingly since Judaism had been in diaspora throughout the Arabian Peninsula since the exile of the sixth century BCE, and Christian communities had been there from at least the early second century CE.

Not much is known about Muhammad's early years. However, he had contact with a man known as Zayd, who was possibly a Christian or a Jew, but he was influential in turning the young man away from the polytheistic faith of Arabia. Muhammad had a particularly religious temperament, and it is said that he habitually went into the hills to practice prayer and meditation, and that at the age of forty he received his prophetic call. The experience of his call is described in the Qur'an, understood as a record of Muhammad's revelations.

One night, as he was in the mountains, the angel Gabriel appeared to him and showed him a text written on silk and commanded him to recite this text. The text is the Qur'an. It is understood by Muslims to be a transcript of the eternal Word of God preserved in heaven. While scholars debate the actual composition of the text, it may well be the case that Muhammad himself is responsible for many of the passages. The entire book is arranged into a number of sections known as *suras*, "revelations." "The Scripture is unique among the sacred books of the great world religions both in the short time lapse between its composition and the establishment of an authoritative tradition, and in its origin from the teaching of a single person."[5]

CHRISTOLOGY

The Qur'an is respectful of Jesus, but it views him as a creature, albeit as a creature who acted through the power of God. "Jesus is nothing but a servant on whom We bestowed favor. We made him an example for the children of Israel" (*Sura* 43:59). Another passage gives us a sense of the honorific titles given to Jesus:

> O People of the Book, be not exaggerated [go beyond proper limits] in your religion; do not utter lies against God, but speak the truth. The Messiah, Jesus the son of Mary, is only a messenger [*rasul*] of God, His word [*kalimah*], which he sent down to Mary and a Spirit from Him. Therefore, believe in God and His messengers and do not say Three! Desist. It is better for you. God is only One. Far be it from Him that he should have a son! To Him

belongs what is in the heavens and on the earth. God is sufficient for a Protector.⁶

Notice the titles given to Jesus in this passage. "Messiah" is a title of honor. He is "word" of God, again a title of honor, but not in the Christian sense of Logos, the incarnate Word of God. Jesus is also a "spirit" from God, but this is to be understood in a creaturely sense, or even perhaps as an angel. The Qur'an has many prophets who ask God's forgiveness and receive that forgiveness. In the case of Jesus, however, there is no mention of his sins, and he is a model of holiness. His miracles are accepted as wondrous permissions of God. Among the miracles that are noted in the Qur'an is the miracle of the bird modeled from clay that Jesus brings to life, taken from the apocryphal *Infancy Gospel of Thomas*.⁷ *Sura* 5 is known as "al-Maida," "the table, the food." In this passage we are told that Jesus asked God to send down from heaven a table set out with food. It may be a reference to the miracle narrative of the multiplication of loaves, and perhaps also to the Last Supper, but there is no sense in this passage of the food being Eucharist as Christians understand it. Finally, Jesus will return at the end of time to complete his earthly life and to die, and this return will be a time of complete peace. Hans Küng offers some helpful comments on the Christology of the Qur'an, citing the scholar Hans-Joachim Schoeps: "While Jewish Christianity in the church came to grief, it was preserved in Islam and, with regard to some of its driving impulses at least, it has lasted till our own time," and then in Küng's own words, "Mohammed's 'christology' may not have been all that different from the christology of the Jewish Christian church."⁸ Küng is referring to the low Christology of some early Jewish-Christian groups that died out before the Council of Nicaea in 325. This perspective certainly has some degree of persuasiveness to it. We have no clear ideas about the length and breadth of the circulation of noncanonical Christian texts in these early centuries. We can be clear, however, that these texts were popular with ordinary people, and reached across the communities of the Middle East.

VATICAN II AND ISLAM

Vatican II's Declaration on the Relationship of the Church to Non-Christian Religions (*Nostra Aetate*) speaks of Muslims in the following way:

> The Church regards with esteem also the Muslims. They adore the one God, living and subsisting in Himself; merciful and all-powerful, the Creator of heaven and earth, who has spoken to men; they take pains to submit wholeheartedly to even His inscrutable decrees, just as Abraham, with whom the faith of Islam takes pleasure in linking itself, submitted to God. Though they do not acknowledge Jesus as God, they revere Him as a prophet. They also honor Mary, His virgin Mother; at times they even call on her with devotion. In addition, they await the day of judgment when God will render their deserts to all those who have been raised up from the dead. Finally, they value the moral life and worship God especially through prayer, almsgiving and fasting. Since in the course of centuries not a few quarrels and hostilities have arisen between Christians and Muslims, this sacred synod urges all to forget the past and to work sincerely for mutual understanding and to preserve as well as to promote together for the benefit of all mankind social justice and moral welfare, as well as peace and freedom.[9]

MARY IN THE CHRISTIAN TRADITION

This text is very important. It acknowledges some of the central tenets of Islam with regard to God. It acknowledges that Jesus has a special place as a prophet of God. It acknowledges the veneration and honor given to the person of Mary, the mother of Jesus. Finally, it acknowledges the "quarrels and hostilities" that have arisen between Muslims and Christians over the centuries and advocates working together for the common good of humankind.

MARY IN ISLAM

"In the absence of a doctrine of incarnation, Islam could not develop a Mariology analogous to the rich evolutions in Christian cultures."[10] Trying to put together what the Qur'an and later Muslim tradition has to say about Mary shows her having an exalted position. God chooses Mary and favors her. She is the daughter of Imran, the father of Moses, Aaron, and Miriam. She is consecrated to God from the moment of her conception, a miraculous conception, and is presented to God in the temple of Jerusalem. An angel appears to her and announces the miraculous conception and birth of a child, Jesus. This child will be a great prophet. Jesus is always referred to as "the son of Mary," and never "the son of God." In Muslim tradition there is a belief that Satan touches all children at birth, but this is not the case with either Jesus or Mary. While there is no hint of the Christian doctrine of original sin in Islam, this gives us a further hint of the high esteem in which Jesus and Mary are held by Muslims. "Abu Huraira (603–81), an important early Muslim scholar, says: I heard the messenger of God say: No descendent of Adam is born but that Satan touches him at birth, except Mary and her son Jesus."[11]

The Qur'an is the sacred text of Islam. "For Muslims it is the literal word of God revealed to their Apostle and Prophet

Muslim Mary

Muhammad on various occasions spanning the last twenty years of his life, ten years in Mecca, and the ten years he lived in Medina after his *hijra* (emigration) from Mecca."[12] The text contains one hundred and fourteen *suras*, or chapters, each with its own particular and traditional title.

The most ancient text referring to Mary is probably *Sura* 19:16–34, known as the *Suryat Maryam*.[13] The text of the *Sura* seems clearly to reflect the immensely popular but noncanonical early second-century Christian text the *Protoevangelium of James*, although, as R. J. McCarthy points out, the Qur'an does not admit of preexisting sources since it is the very word of God revealed directly to Muhammad. Once again, the *Sura* echoes the words of the episode of the angel Gabriel's annunciation to Mary in Luke 2:26–38. Mary's response to the angel ("How can this be since I am a virgin?") finds expression in slightly different words in the *Sura*, followed by Gabriel's proclamation of the Holy Spirit "overshadowing" Mary.[14] There is in this text, then, a reverential and deeply Christian appreciation of Mary. However, and as one might expect, the *Sura* reflects what Christians would call a "low Christology," in other words, a view of Jesus that acknowledges him to be a prophet, the servant of God, but not obviously divine. The same "low Christology" may be found in other texts in the Qur'an.[15]

CONCLUSION

"Mary offered an attractive point of intersection: dear to Christians, cherished by Muslims, derided by Jews, she was a figure that sparked the imagination."[16] "Derided by Jews"— that may have been the case in earlier centuries, not so today in these more ecumenical times. The scholarly work of the Jewish New Testament expert Amy-Jill Levine, for example, leads to a much more positive and constructive approach to the person of Mary.[17] What about a more positive and constructive approach to Mary from the perspective of Islam? The comments of the Catholic Muslim scholar R. J. McCarthy are helpful here: "In the case of Islamo-Christian dialogue it seems that the position of Mary in Islam and the veneration which many Muslims have for her are elements which can contribute to what we may term a friendly climate....But the realization of a fruitful dialogue will take time and much patience and most of all great and sincere love. In this Mary, though she may not be a touchstone, may well be a stepping-stone. Certainly she will not be a stumbling block."[18] This is a good way to end our brief Muslim snapshot of Mary.

7

MEDIEVAL MARY

St. Bernard of Clairvaux, St. Thomas Aquinas, and Bl. Duns Scotus

It would be true to say that in the medieval period of the Latin West we find a certain golden age of Mariology. Devotion to Mary flourished ubiquitously in so many different ways, at so many different local centers, and theological reflection on Mary made rapid progress in monastic, scholastic and vernacular theological circles.

Historical theologian David Bell has it correct when he writes, "It is difficult to exaggerate either the importance or the popularity of the Mother of God in the Middle Ages. Much of it, of course, is understandable. All children, if they are lost or sad or hurt or in trouble, want their mothers, and the children of God are no different. Mary provided a feminine face for an all too masculine deity, and the compassion, love, availability, approachability, warmth, consolation, and comfort that we all like to associate with a loving mother were found in the Mother of God."[1]

During the period that we know as the High Middle Ages, there was a growing emphasis in Christian communities on the humanity of Christ—to take only two examples, St. Francis of Assisi and the Franciscan emphasis on the Christmas crib displaying Christ as a newborn infant, and the many meditative devotions to the Good Friday moments of the passion of Christ as the Stations of the Cross. Allied to this emphasis on Christ's humanity was increased attention to the virtues of our Lady and to theological speculation about her. "The center of attention of believers shifted from Mary as representing the faithful church, and so also redeemed humanity, to Mary as dispensing Christ's graces to the faithful....Mary came widely to be viewed as an intermediary between God and humanity, and even as a worker of miracles with powers that verged on the divine. This popular piety in due course influenced the theological opinions of those who had grown up with it, and who subsequently elaborated a theological rationale for the florid Marian devotion of the Late Middle Ages."[2] Mary becomes in a sense a dominant figure from the eleventh through the thirteenth centuries, both in terms of popular devotion and also theological reflection. If it was devotion to Mary that carried forward the themes and ideas of Marian theology in the patristic period, it was the same widespread and popular devotion that became omnipresent in the medieval Christian world, and sometimes popular devotion in contrast to academic theology. In this particular medieval snapshot, brief attention will be given to three theologians, St. Bernard of Clairvaux, St. Thomas Aquinas, and Bl. John Duns Scotus.

Medieval Mary

ST. BERNARD OF CLAIRVAUX (1090-1153)

"In the twelfth century, Bernard was the author who dominated the field of Marian thought. Even though the Marian contents of his many works are not particularly abundant, he had a remarkable gift for speaking about the Blessed Virgin in a fascinating way. Tradition has named him the 'Champion and Singer of the Virgin.'"[3] Bernard picked up a key medieval Marian theme that since Christ came to us through Mary, we come to Christ through her. "Let us venerate Mary with the whole of our hearts, with all our most intimate affections and desires, for this is the will [of God], who has willed that we have everything through Mary."[4]

Bernard also reiterated the notion that Mary, "full of grace" (Luke 1:28), had never sinned and, in fact, had been given by God the privilege of being sinless from the first moment of her conception. While most theologians of the time would have accepted that Mary had never sinned, it was far from universally agreed that she had been conceived without original sin, that is say, that Mary was conceived immaculately—the immaculate conception, as it came to be called. Bernard certainly did not believe in the immaculate conception of Mary precisely in those terms, but he certainly believed that she was sinless. "Something had to have happened between the moment of her conception and her birth. Sometime during that period she was cleansed from original sin by a specific act of God's grace, and it was when she was *born*, not when she was conceived, that she was unstained and immaculate."[5] In other words, for Bernard, and for many others, and as a result of the Augustinian doctrine of original sin, Mary was conceived in sin but by God's grace cleansed of original sin before her birth. It may seem a matter of little importance today but at the time what was at stake was the universality of redemption brought about by Jesus Christ. If that redemption brought about by Christ was to include the whole world, then that also had to include Mary and thus, she was conceived in the state of original sin but cleansed of it by the grace of God prior to her birth.

For Bernard Mary becomes the aqueduct between heaven and humankind, the aqueduct that carries our divine adoption and divinization. That, of course, is effected by Christ, but his coming to be one of us, what we are, his coming from heaven to earth required a passage, so to speak, a life-giving passage, like the passage of water through an aqueduct. "Mary is like an aqueduct that was able to reach the lofty springs of divine grace and convey it to the faithful on earth by the force of her desire, the fervor of her piety, and the purity of her prayer."[6]

When it comes to the assumption of Mary, Bernard "seems deliberately to have left it in the dark."[7] The Marian historian and theologian Hilda Graef maintains that although Bernard has left four sermons on the Feast of the Assumption of Mary, "he never affirmed that he believed Mary to be in heaven with her body." Despite the constancy of his teaching and his obvious commitment to the Virgin Mary, both temperamentally and theologically Bernard was opposed to anything that smacked to him of "originality of thought"—hence his opposition to what he considered the theological novelties of Peter Abelard—and so, while honoring the Virgin, he could not go so far as to affirm that the final resurrection of the dead had occurred for her.[8] And so in his sermons on the assumption he speaks about Mary being received into heaven and about her intercession for the Church, but he remains hesitant about her bodily assumption. Bernard writes, "I have learned from the church to celebrate with the greatest veneration this day, on which the Virgin, taken up from the wicked world, caused the most splendid and joyful festival in heaven."[9]

ST. THOMAS AQUINAS (1225-1274)

Despite St. Thomas's massive theological output, he does not in his writing devote much attention to the Blessed Virgin Mary. His Marian reflection is "thoroughly incorporated into his Christology."[10] With this principle firmly in mind for St. Thomas, Mary was sanctified in the womb but before animation, that is to say before her body received her soul. This form of expression may seem a little strange to us today, but in St. Thomas's analysis of the person there is "some interval of time between conception and the infusion of the soul."[11] Thomas cannot accept the notion of Mary's immaculate conception although, like St. Bernard, he maintains her freedom from sin. Thus, he is not opposed to celebrating the conception of Mary since that conception was celebrated in various churches at the time, but he comments as follows: "Since the time that she was sanctified is unknown the feast of her sanctification rather than her conception is celebrated on the day of her conception."[12]

BL. JOHN DUNS SCOTUS (CA. 1266-1308)

Hilda Graef offers us a great introduction to the Franciscan theologian Duns Scotus. "Duns Scotus was a philosopher and theologian, not a preacher or a devotional writer, hence he has no time for the absurdities...of popular authors." What absurdities did Graef have in mind? She continues, "He denied that the Blessed Virgin, sinless as she was, had ever gone to confession, and that she had received the graces of the priesthood; nor could he accept that she could give orders to God."[13] In describing Scotus in this way Graef is showing us, consciously or not, how orthodox systematic theology can be a corrective over against well-intentioned popular devotions.

Scotus differed from St. Bernard when it came to the immaculate conception. The principal theological objection to the immaculate conception of our Lady was that it seemed to be incompatible with the universal scope of the redemption brought about by Christ. If Mary was immaculately conceived, that is without sin, then she did not need redemption. Scotus's response to this theological objection was that "a redemption that preserves from sin is more perfect than one that frees from it," or, in more contemporary language "prevention is better than cure." The redemption brought about by Christ was anticipated for Mary, not that she did not need it. He termed this anticipation "pre-redemption." The most perfect method of redemption, as it were, was to preserve our Blessed Lady from original sin rather than to rescue her from it.[14]

CONCLUSION

Local devotions to our Blessed Lady are to be found everywhere throughout medieval Europe, and, of course, from there they were taken to the New World of the Americas. In this chapter attention has been restricted to three medieval theologians. Standing back somewhat from the narrative I think it is possible to detect a certain inevitable tension between what we might refer to as the excessive devotional attention to Mary among the ordinary Christian people and academic theological reflection. For a growing number of academic theologians the popular devotional attention given to Mary seemed to take away from the centrality of our Lord, and the desire grew to right this imbalance. That desire leads us to the reformers of the sixteenth century. We read in the ecumenical Anglican-Roman Catholic Seattle Statement on Mary the following:

> One powerful impulse for Reformation in the early sixteenth century was a widespread reaction against devotional practices which approached Mary as a mediatrix alongside Christ, or sometimes even in his place....Together with a radical re-reception of Scripture as the fundamental touchstone of divine revelation, there was a re-reception by the Reformers of the belief that Jesus Christ is the only mediator between God and humanity.[15]

While this remains an entirely accurate comment with regard to the Reformation, the classical Reformers themselves did not simply abandon devotion to Mary, and it is to these that we now turn in the next chapter.

8
MARY AND THE REFORMERS

> The widespread assertion that the Reformers ignored the Virgin Mary and had no Mariology is not tenable.
>
> George Tavard[1]

> The Roman Catholic response (to Protestant views of Mary) was often disdainful, disregarding deeply felt criticisms that were not without some genuine foundations.
>
> Christopher O'Donnell[2]

INTRODUCTION

In his classic *Civilization: A Personal View*, Kenneth Clark made the following observation:

> And so Protestantism became destructive, and from the point of view of those who love what they see, was an unmitigated disaster....We all know about

the destruction of images...how commissioners went round to even the humblest parish church and smashed everything of beauty it contained.... You can see the results in almost every old church and cathedral in England, and a good many in France. For example, in the Lady Chapel at Ely, all the glass was smashed, and as the beautiful series of carvings of the life of the Virgin was in reach they knocked off every head—made a thorough job of it. I suppose the motive wasn't so much religious as an instinct to destroy anything comely, anything that reflected a state of mind that an unevolved man could not share.[3]

On the one hand, the late Catholic ecumenical theologian George Tavard points out that the Reformers did not ignore the Virgin Mary and that they had a Mariology. On the other hand, Clark points out the devastating iconoclasm of the Reformation, perhaps with a degree of acerbity. It is something of a paradox that both are correct. Our concern, however, will be more with Tavard than with Clark.

LUTHER, CALVIN, AND ZWINGLI

It hardly needs to be pointed out that as his thinking and reflection developed on all the central aspects of traditional Catholic doctrine, Martin Luther reacted negatively to everything that smacked to him of superstition and exaggeration. One author describes Luther's negative reaction to Marian devotion in these terms:

> He went to Rome in the early 1501, and as he made the usual pilgrimages through the city, he was shown some milk from the Virgin's breast and some of

Mary's hair. No doubt he must have heard again the words which had repeated themselves in his mind as he climbed the Scala Sancta: "Who knows whether this is true?"...There is no doubt that these abuses within the church were a cause of the rapid success of Luther's preaching.[4]

It would be incorrect, however, to view his understanding of Mary simply in negative terms responding to naïve popular religiosity and superstition. "Much to the astonishment of many Protestants and Catholics, it is on the topic of the praise of and devotion to Mary that the Reformers were most outspoken."[5] Luther's understanding of Mary was very real, and was expressed in hymns that he composed, albeit strongly theocentric and christocentric hymns. She is for him the foremost example of the grace of God, and everyone is utterly dependent upon God's grace. "His aim is not to exalt Mary; it is precisely her humility that is emphasized, in order to praise the greatness of the act of God's mercy. It was through grace that she became the Mother of God, not through merit!"[6] In a sermon preached in 1516, just one year prior to his famous 1517 theses, Luther wrote as follows:

> The Blessed Virgin sees God in all things....Although Elizabeth with great perception sees Mary to be the Mother of God, even more perceptively the Virgin sees God in all things; he alone is great. Therefore the most pure generator of God is the Blessed Virgin, who magnifies God above all things; she has no idols. She boasts of nothing herself, nothing of merit, no work; she is, by her own admission, purely passive and a receiver, not a doer of good works.[7]

Mary and the Reformers

Already we can see here prior to his protest Luther's emphasis that salvation is God's free and gratuitous gift, in no way dependent on human work or effort. Mary is the premier exemplar of receptivity to God's gift. In similar fashion consider this passage from his 1521 *Commentary on the Magnificat*: "I say Mary does not desire to be an idol; she does nothing; God does all. We ought to call upon her that for her sake God may grant and do what we request. Thus also, all other saints are to be invoked, so that their work may be every way God's alone."[8] The words "God does all" form the centerpiece of Luther's theology. Everything to do with our salvation is the free gift of God alone, and has nothing to do with what we do, nothing to do with any of our own personal merits. Here is a very fine summary of Luther's commentary:

> It is becoming evident that the novelty of Luther's approach to Mary is that he focuses on what God achieves in her, and not on her own achievements. He highlights what God does in her, and not what she herself does. For Luther, Mary's response to God models what our response should be, because she opens herself completely to the mystery of God. The greatness of Mary is in her huge and grateful yes of faith, her surrender to God's loving plan for her. Luther places before our admiring gaze this self-effacing woman from Nazareth, who combines deep humility with complete trust in God. She is small enough and trusting enough to open herself to the unimaginable fullness of God's grace.[9]

When Luther's commentary was published, it is said that Pope Leo X—the very same pope who had excommunicated Luther—read the commentary and said, "Blessed are the hands that have written this."[10] Luther's understanding of

Mary is also intended to be a clear corrective to what he took to be popular misunderstandings, misrepresentations, or perhaps sheer superstitions of his day with regard to Mary and the saints.

"Luther's warmth towards Mary continued to be expressed in his preaching, which remained tied to the liturgical year, because he kept so much more of the calendar than other churches in the Protestant world. Free to choose which he would retain of the festivals associated with Mary, he kept those which could be seen as centering on Christ rather than Mary: The Annunciation, the Visitation, the Purification."[11] Luther also loved the Magnificat, and so the Feast of the Visitation was especially important for him. Was Luther an iconoclast like so many others in the Reformation tradition? Writing around the time of Vatican II and having done considerable research into Marian theology in the Reformation tradition, Thomas O'Meara concludes that he was not an iconoclast. "Iconoclasm was a byproduct of the Reformation which Luther strictly forbade. He rightly criticizes certain paintings of Mary where Christ is portrayed as a stern judge held back from the destruction of sinners only by Mary. These, Luther advises the people, should be destroyed." Finally, O'Meara reports that "some authorities think that Luther himself had a picture of Mary hanging in his room."[12]

In somewhat similar fashion to Martin Luther, John Calvin affirmed that everything must be understood in the light of the majesty and glory of God. God is first, foremost and center always. Calvin was mariologically the minimalist among the Reformers, in O'Meara's words "Calvin treats Mary only in passing."[13] For Calvin, Rome had made an idol of Mary and so in Calvin's city of Geneva all festivals of Mary were suppressed. Nonetheless, he maintains that "the greatest devotion we can give to Mary is if we follow her in discipleship and acknowledge her as our example and teacher,"[14] in some

Mary and the Reformers

ways anticipating themes in Vatican II's Constitution on the Church in the final chapter on our Lady.

The third of the classic trio of Reformers, Huldrych Zwingli's Mariology has been thus described:

> Mary is an instrument of salvation-history, and a *model* of Christian life, a *sign* and a *witness*, who points to the miracle and mystery of Christ.... Zwingli also retains to the last the Marian festivals, but decisively opposes the religious veneration of Mary, and strictly forbids men to worship her, even to call upon her. True honor is done to Mary by caring for the poor.[15]

To illustrate Zwingli's position, let us turn to the account of a Franciscan friar from Avignon in France, François Lambert, who had composed a popular devotional work with the title *The Crown of Our Savior Jesus Christ* about 1520. Though patterned on the rosary and containing prayers to Mary as well as the angels and saints for their intercession, Lambert had changed the focus from Mary to the mysteries of Christ's life. In 1522, Lambert was in the Zürich church known as the Fraumünster preaching on the intercession of Mary and the saints. During the sermon he was heckled by Huldrych Zwingli with the words, "Brother, that's where you're wrong." The next day he debated with Zwingli. The outcome was Lambert's abandonment of the Franciscan habit and his championing of the cause of the Reformation. The episode witnesses not only to Zwingli's anti-Marian sentiments, at least to her intercession, but perhaps also to the persuasiveness for many of his point of view.[16] At the same time, amongst the Reformers Zwingli was the one who was most socially and politically aware. So, when the question is raised about how properly to praise Mary, this is his response:

Not with candles, incense, hymns and the like. Mary is not poor. She does not need money. She is extremely rich in every respect; she does not need us. She does not need treasures, not even special Marian churches. But she needs to be honored in the women and daughters of the earth. We praise her by spending the money we would otherwise spend on candles, to enhance the dignity of poor daughters and women whose beauty is endangered by poverty.[17]

Having taken all of these qualifying comments into consideration, one may still say that, in summary, the Protestant contribution was to prune away excess, to eliminate the medieval mariological axiom "of Mary never enough can be said." That leaves a reduced Mariology, but a Mariology it still is. "'Mary' must be defended from becoming the product of our pious imagination....The most important fruit of a Protestant contribution might then well be, that behind the rank foliage of a mystical and uncontrolled 'Mariology,' the real picture of our Lord's mother would be revealed in a new astringency, simplicity, beauty."[18]

TURNING TO THE TWENTIETH CENTURY WITH JOHN MACQUARRIE

The Anglican theologian John Macquarrie represents a kind of Protestant maximalism when it comes to the Blessed Virgin Mary.[19] John Macquarrie (1919–2007) writes, "No ecumenical theology could afford to ignore [Mariology]."[20] Although in the earlier years of the English Reformation there was a strong reaction against what were understood to be the excesses of Marian piety and devotion, throughout the centuries of the

Mary and the Reformers

Anglican Communion and especially since the time of the Oxford Movement of the mid-nineteenth century, there has been a greater appreciation of our Lady among many Anglican theologians, among whom John Macquarrie has a certain well-established pride of place.[21]

A hymn to our Lady composed by Macquarrie in 1966, just one year after the end of Vatican II and Pope St. Paul VI's proclamation of Mary as "Mother of the Church," is also entitled "Mother of the Church."[22] The hymn witnesses to Macquarrie's growing Marian devotion around the time of the publication of his very influential theological *summa*, *Principles of Christian Theology*. The content of the hymn is essentially this: "What we see in Mary, we ought to see in the Church."[23]

In his *Principles of Christian Theology* Macquarrie treats of Mary in the chapter devoted to ecclesiology. He recognizes right away that his inclusion of this topic in a book on systematic theology may stir a negative reaction among those of a Protestant background, and so immediately he reassures by saying that his treatment will be roundly based on Sacred Scripture, respecting the *sola scriptura* emphasis of the Reformation tradition.[24] If one begins with Scripture one sees that the discovery of the "historical Mary" is even more fraught with problems and difficulties than the "historical Jesus." In the Gospel records as we now have them the narrative is a mixture of historical and legendary material. The data presented offer us truths of faith, not raw historical fact, and perhaps are best designated as "mysteries." Macquarrie considers three of these Marian mysteries: the annunciation, the visitation, and the station at the cross. The annunciation, emphasizing the initiative of God, reveals the incarnation taking place through the action of the Holy Spirit. It has also a contemporary meaning in that something similar happens in and to the Church: "for just as [Mary] was the bearer of the Christ, so the church, his body, brings christhood into the world...through the action of the Holy Spirit...."[25] The visitation of Mary to Elizabeth was the occasion for the great canticle of the Magnificat. The key word in the canticle is "Blessed." Blessed among women, according to Elizabeth's greeting and blessed by all generations, Mary is indeed the blessed one. Her blessedness, however, "adumbrates the blessedness of the church—no earthly happiness, but a 'likeness to God' which means a participation in God's self-giving love."[26] Mary's blessedness in the visitation mystery is a type also of the blessedness of the Church. It expresses something of the Church's vocation. The third mystery, Mary's station at the cross, too contains an ecclesial aspect. Relying on an insight of the Danish theologian-philosopher Søren Kierkegaard, Macquarrie points out that Mary's suffering is not to be understood "as only a natural grief at the sight of Jesus' death, but as a sharing in his self-emptying, as if Mary were experiencing something of what Christ expressed in his cry of dereliction; and Mary's suffering is experienced in turn by every disciple."[27] In these three mysteries Mary is closely linked to the Church, and this is where, according to Macquarrie, she is best understood.

The best clue to the scriptural understanding of Mary is the title given to her by Pope Paul VI, "Mother of the Church," essentially the substance of Macquarrie's 1966 hymn to Mary. This title, Macquarrie believes, provides an opening on which Catholics, Orthodox, Anglicans, and Protestants may agree. It is an ecumenically accessible title for Mary. Its scriptural basis may be found on the lips of Jesus on the cross, "Woman, here is your son....Here is your mother!" (John 19:26). Behind the title there lie two meanings. First, it accords to Mary "a certain priority in the church, as one who played an indispensable role in the Christian drama of incarnation and salvation."[28] The second meaning behind the title is Mary as the prototype

Mary and the Reformers

of the Church: "What we see in Mary, we ought to see in the church."[29]

CONCLUSION

The sixteenth-century Reformers had a Mariology but what may be termed a chastened Mariology, and moreover one that places our Lady firmly within the Church. If we move on to our contemporary ecumenical context, we may recognize not only elements of this chastened Mariology but also a more constructive and positive theology of Mary. A veteran ecumenical theologian David Carter makes an important point when he says this: "A key feature of the last decades of the previous century and first decade of this has been an increasing degree of interest taken by a minority of Protestant theologians and spiritual writers in Mary; how far their work...will be more generally 'received' within their churches remains to be seen."[30] Reception by the ordinary faithful of the churches in respect of our Lady represents no small challenge. However, whatever shapes the ongoing search for greater Christian unity may take, it seems quite certain that there continues to be a place for the veneration of Mary and for Mariology within the Reformed ecclesial traditions.

9
MARY IN VATICAN II'S CONSTITUTION ON THE CHURCH

> Any viable modern Catholic restatement of Mariological teaching must take the Second Vatican Council's teaching as its starting point.
>
> Eamon Duffy[1]

> Chapter 8 of *Lumen Gentium* is in a certain sense a magna carta of the Mariology of our era.
>
> Pope St. John Paul II, Discourse at General Audience, May 2, 1979

BRIEF SUMMARY PRIOR TO VATICAN II

Both the nineteenth and twentieth centuries are marked by great devotion to our Blessed Lady and by an enormous amount of Marian publications. However, according to the Irish Carmelite theologian Christopher O'Donnell, "the study of Mary became divorced from the mainstream of theology,

Mary in Vatican II's Constitution on the Church

and...Mariology became the realm of specialists."[2] Mariologists, the specialists writing about our Blessed Lady, became in O'Donnell's words "maximalists" or "minimalists." O'Donnell continues, "The former desired more feasts, new definitions, more devotions; they were very interested in apparitions and were somewhat less than critical in their use of the Scripture and patristic writings. The latter tended to want to develop existing doctrines and feasts, to be more stringent in their use of Scripture and patristic writings, and on the whole to be more ecumenically sensitive, with less interest in apparitions."[3] O'Donnell concludes as follows: "[This division between maximalists and minimalists by the late 1950s may be understood as] the recognition of two different emphases in writing: a Christotypical one, in which all of the mysteries were seen more in relation to Christ; and ecclesiotypical one in which the Marian dogmas were primarily seen in their relation to the church."[4] O'Donnell, an important contributor to Mariology himself, has provided us here with a balanced summary of reflection on Mary on the cusp of Vatican II.[5]

The maximalist Mariologists of the period after the Council of Trent (1545-63) and especially of the nineteenth and twentieth centuries developed what might be called an "isolated Mariology...a deductive type of Mariology that was centered on Mary and her privileges, and had a tendency to foster marian titles and dogmas, and was closed to dialogue with our brothers of the Reformed tradition."[6] Many in the Reformed tradition were of the opinion that Catholics worshiped Mary. Of course, that was never the case, a strong distinction was made between the worship/*latreia* that was due to God alone, and to the devotion and veneration/*hyperdulia* that the faithful offered to Mary. Vatican II's Constitution on the Church remarks that "this cult, as it has always existed in the Church, for all its uniqueness, differs essentially from the cult of adoration, which is offered equally to the Incarnate

Word and to the Father and the Holy Spirit, and it is most favorable to it" (no. 66). The very fact, however, that Protestants thought that Catholics worshiped Mary seems to point to something that they considered to be at least an imbalance, or an excessive emphasis in the Catholic tradition. Perhaps we may describe the traditional Catholic position in terms already introduced as "Marian maximalism" and the traditional Protestant position as "Marian minimalism." If those categories seem basically fair, then Vatican II's Constitution on the Church, chapter 8, that deals with the Blessed Virgin Mary seems to strike a very fine balance between these two points of view.

VATICAN II

In chapter 8 of Vatican II's Constitution on the Church we find the conciliar understanding of our Lady. In this text we may see the christotypical emphasis and the ecclesiotypical emphasis on Mary being placed in a kind of parallel fashion side by side, "though with some overlapping."[7] Paragraphs 55–59 may be seen as primarily christotypical and 60–65 as ecclesiotypical.

In reaching what we might understand as this Marian balance, Vatican II developed a Mariology that is biblical, ecclesial, and ecumenical. Right away in paragraph 52 of the Constitution we read, "Joined to Christ the head and in communion with all his saints, the faithful must in the first place reverence the memory of the glorious ever Virgin Mary, Mother of God and of our Lord Jesus Christ." In this statement we can recognize a christocentric emphasis alongside the clear acknowledgment of Mary within the Communion of Saints, in many ways a retrieval of patristic theology. The christocentric emphasis is taken further in paragraph 62: "The Blessed Virgin is invoked in the Church under the titles of

Mary in Vatican II's Constitution on the Church

Advocate, Helper, Benefactress, and Mediatrix. This, however, is so understood that it neither takes away anything from nor adds anything to the dignity and efficacy of Christ the one Mediator." Here we can see very clearly an ecumenical motive at work, commending the veneration of the Blessed Virgin Mary while at the same time insisting that her Son is the sole mediator of salvation. Furthermore, Mary is hailed "as pre-eminent and as a wholly unique member of the Church, and as its type and outstanding model in faith and charity" (no. 53). The ecclesiotypical emphasis proceeds in developing Mary's maternity (nos. 60–61), her being associate and handmaid of the Redeemer (no. 61), intercessor (no. 62), and finally as type and model of the Church (nos. 63–65). So now we have not only a christocentric emphasis but also an ecclesiocentric emphasis. Mary is seen as a type and model of the Church, again a theme dear to patristic theology.

Turning briefly to the Constitution on the Sacred Liturgy from Vatican II we find the following statement with regard to our Blessed Lady: "While it celebrates this annual round of the events of Christ's sacramental life and work, holy church gives honor to Mary the mother of God, with a quite special love. She is inseparably linked to the saving work of her Son; in her, the church admires and holds up the outstanding result of the redemption, and joyfully contemplates what is, as it were, a totally undistorted picture of its desires and hopes for itself as a whole" (no. 103). Christotypical and ecclesiotypical thinking about Mary come together in liturgical celebration.

ECUMENICAL APPRECIATION OF MARY AFTER VATICAN II

This Marian development flowing from Vatican II is arguably one of the factors that has contributed to a growing appreciation of Mary in the Reformation tradition. It may be helpful at this point to acknowledge some comments of the Lutheran theologian, Robert W. Jenson, who writes of Mary,

> There must be a mysterious sense in which Mary *is* heaven, the container not only of the uncontainable Son, but of all his sisters and brothers, of what Augustine called the *totus Christus*, the whole Christ, Christ with his body. But Mary is a person, not a sheer container. That she contains the whole company of heaven must mean that she personally is their presence. To ask Mary to pray for us is to ask "the whole company of heaven" to pray for us, not this saint or that but all of them together. It is to ask the church triumphant to pray for us.[8]

What a beautiful statement bringing together Christology and Mariology. Another Lutheran theologian, David S. Yeago, has written, and, moreover, has written out of a very clear scriptural perspective concerning Mary, "Mary is irreducibly *present* within the redemptive relationship of the church and of the believer to Christ, not merely as a symbolic figure but as a particular person; there is no redemptive relationship to Jesus Christ that does not contain within itself a relationship to Mary, though not, of course, the *same* relationship."[9] For Yeago, out of this scriptural perspective, Mary emerges as the prototype and model of the Church and even as an active agent in the life of the believer, a very firm and strong ecclesiocentric emphasis.

I think that this kind of perspective from a Lutheran would have been impossible prior to Vatican II. The council's mandate to Roman Catholics to be involved in ecumenism in all its dimensions was the catalyst for all manner of theological dialogues about issues that have traditionally been divisive, and yet, as we have seen in the chapter on the Reformers, Mary is not alien to a Lutheran spirituality and theology. Indeed, it could be argued that theologians such as Jenson and Yeago are creatively and imaginatively, and as a result ecumenically, retrieving a very practical Mariology. That is why Yeago goes on to suggest that local retrieval of Mariology for Lutherans—and, one suspects, for other Christians in the traditions of the Reformation—could be enabled by attending to the annual feasts of Mary in the liturgical calendar and by singing the Magnificat, which Luther considered should be sung twice a day![10]

CONCLUSION

The Second Vatican Council came to an end in 1965, and since that time there have been many developments in Catholic theology and devotion. The liturgy has been transformed from Latin into all the vernacular languages, with massive popular appeal. The move from a seemingly christotypical approach to our Blessed Lady to include also an ecclesiotypical approach has meant for many, albeit probably unintentionally, a lessening of interest in Mary. That was never the intention of the council, but perhaps it may also have led to a more balanced position with regard to our Blessed Lady. At the same time, we also have to acknowledge the greater appreciation for Mary in the churches of the Reformation tradition, a very definite gain from Vatican II's emphasis on ecumenism.

10

THE MARIAN DOGMAS
The Immaculate Conception and the Assumption

> Time and time again ecumenical discussion about Mary comes up against the two recent Marian dogmas of the Immaculate Conception (1854) and the Assumption (1950).
>
> Christopher O'Donnell[1]

THE DOGMA OF THE IMMACULATE CONCEPTION

In a fine reflection on the immaculate conception the Dominican theologian Herbert McCabe begins with these words: "What we celebrate on December 8 is not, of course, a feast of the doctrine of the Immaculate Conception; we do not have feasts of doctrines, we celebrate the gift of God where it is to be found, in people. On this feast we celebrate Mary as conceived without sin."[2] McCabe is making a very helpful point here, that is to say, that we celebrate Mary and not doctrines

The Marian Dogmas

about her. This is not about diminishing the importance of doctrine—they are always important and necessarily so—but rather it is about acknowledging the centrality of worship, liturgy, and devotion.

In 1854, Pope Pius IX in the bull *Ineffabilis Deus* proclaimed the dogma of the immaculate conception of Mary in these words: "We declare...that the most blessed Virgin Mary in the first moment of her conception was, by the unique grace and privilege of God, in view of the merits of Jesus Christ the Savior of the human race, preserved intact from all stain of original sin."

With this act, a belief with a long history in the Church, but which was also the subject of considerable controversy, became official Catholic doctrine. In the chapter on "Medieval Mary" we have seen both the growth in devotion to our Lady and at the same time a certain theological reluctance about the immaculate conception, Mary's freedom from original sin, although not about her sinlessness. The Scriptures are always received in the Church in that process of reception that we know as tradition, the very act of the Church perpetuating itself down through the ages until the end of time. Early in that process of traditioning itself, members of the Church witnessed to Mary's holiness in view of her Son, and the notion that she was always free from sin is a consequence of that witness.

Closer to our own times, the belief in Mary's immaculate conception grew in strength among the faithful. In nineteenth-century France, for example, the visions of St. Catherine Labouré and St. Bernadette Soubirous focused on the belief. On December 17, 1830, Catherine Labouré, a Daughter of Charity of St. Vincent de Paul, had a vision of the blessed Virgin standing on a globe, her hands giving out rays of light, spreading out toward the earth. The vision was surrounded by an oval frame on which were found the words "O Mary, conceived without sin, pray for us who have recourse to thee." Catherine heard a voice asking that a medal be struck like the model she had seen in her vision. This became known as the "Miraculous Medal," because of many miracles attributed to it. This experience stimulated interest in the immaculate conception, and increased demands for the definition of the doctrine. Similarly, on February 11, 1858, Bernadette Soubirous began to have visions of a beautiful lady at Massabielle, Lourdes. Asking the lady for her name, Bernadette was told, "I am the Immaculate Conception."

This nineteenth-century flourishing of the belief in the immaculate conception is not the whole story, a story too complex to rehearse in its entirety here. So, let us focus on some of the highlights. The doctrine of original sin, to which the immaculate conception necessarily relates, became widespread after the formulation given to it by St. Augustine of Hippo. For Augustine original sin is transmitted through paternal generation, following from an androcentric biology, and it leads to a contamination of the fetus, what he called "the infection of the flesh," which affected the rational soul at its infusion. That way of looking at the human person clearly and immediately led to significant problems with Mary, whose cult was growing at the time. Did her father pass on original sin to her who was to become Mother of God? Augustine did not wish to answer this question in the affirmative, but he did not develop an especially clear response. In a quite famous passage, he writes,

> We must make an exception of the holy Virgin Mary, concerning whom I wish to raise no question when it touches the subject of sins, out of honor to the Lord. For from him we know what abundance of grace for overcoming every sin in every particular

The Marian Dogmas

was conferred upon her who had the merit to conceive and bear him who undoubtedly had no sin.[3]

On one level, his words here come very close to saying that Mary is free of original sin, making of Mary "the great exception." On another level, however, his understanding of human concupiscence will not permit it. "His understanding of concupiscence as an integral part of all marital relations made it difficult, if not impossible, to accept that she herself was conceived immaculately."[4] From this time onward, there is a constant tension in the tradition between affirming Mary's freedom from original sin, mainly as a mark of the popular devotion that is intrinsic to the devotional sense of the ordinary faithful, and denying this freedom as making the redemption brought by the Lord redundant vis-à-vis Mary.

The great scholastic theologians of the Middle Ages made a distinction between conception and animation, something we have already touched upon in the chapter on "Medieval Mary." In scholastic thinking conception is what takes place when a pregnancy occurs, while animation is the infusion of the rational soul. In general, the scholastics thought that Mary incurred the Augustinian "infection of the flesh," since she was conceived in the normal human way, but she was then sanctified by means of a special, divine, purifying intervention that occurred in two stages. The first stage was in the womb, and just after animation. This stage consisted in Mary's being freed from all actual sin, including venial sin. The second stage was at the conception of Jesus, at which point she was completely freed from original sin. Here is how the greatest of the medieval scholastics, St. Thomas Aquinas, viewed this issue:

> The sanctification of the Blessed Virgin cannot be understood as having taken place before animation

> for two reasons. First, because the sanctification of which we are speaking, is nothing but the cleansing from original sin....Now sin cannot be taken away except by grace, the subject of which is the rational creature alone. Therefore, before the infusion of the rational soul, the Blessed Virgin was not sanctified. Secondly, because, since the rational creature alone can be the subject of sin; before the infusion of the rational soul, the offspring conceived is not liable to sin. And thus, in whatever manner the Blessed Virgin would have been sanctified before animation, she could never have incurred the stain of original sin: and thus she would not have needed redemption and salvation which is by Christ....It remains, therefore, that the Blessed Virgin was sanctified after animation.[5]

Thomas seems to assume some time between pregnancy and animation or the infusion of the rational soul. If Mary was conceived without original sin, she did not need redemption, which is clearly wrong. At the same time, it was entirely appropriate that Mary should be free of all sin, original and actual, and this special freedom from original sin occurred after animation.

As already acknowledged the Scottish Franciscan theologian John Duns Scotus (1266–1308) took this developing tradition about Mary's immaculate conception further by positing that conception and animation are simultaneous. Thus, Mary is preserved from original sin at the very moment of conception. Scotus's axiom here is that prevention is better than cure.

Vladimir Lossky (1903–58), the twentieth-century Orthodox theologian, represents the typical Eastern Orthodox approach to the immaculate conception: "The dogma of the

Immaculate Conception is foreign to the Eastern tradition, which does not want to separate the Holy Virgin from the sons of Adam."[6] The connection of Mary with "the sons of Adam" is important to Lossky because he wishes to avoid at all costs any kind of docetism in her regard. Mary is a real human being, and the immaculate conception seems to suggest that her humanity is less than fully real. While Lossky's point is well taken as a salutary warning in thinking about Mary, it does not seem particularly cogent in respect of the immaculate conception. As John Macquarrie points out, "A docetic understanding of Mary would be just as intolerable as a docetic understanding of Christ....[The immaculate conception] does not imply any separation of Mary from the human race or any break in her descent from her human ancestors."[7] It may be, however, that the way devotion to Mary as the immaculate conception is sometimes expressed, could give the impression of a docetic Mary. Indeed, it is hard to avoid this given the central place she holds in the lives of Catholics, but as Macquarrie indicates, docetism is entirely unhelpful, either in respect of our Lord or our Lady.

UNDERSTANDING THE DOGMA[8]

In the dogma of the immaculate conception there are two basic ideas, "conception" and "immaculate." *Conception* means "the absolute origination of a person."[9] According to Macquarrie, the conception of Mary may be considered in three contexts: in the mind of God, in the people of Israel, and in the marriage relationship of Mary's parents. This is a useful theological method for teasing out the initial meaning of the dogma.

First, in the mind of God. Think of a passage from the Old Testament that is often applied to Mary, Proverbs 8:22ff.:

"The LORD created me at the beginning of his work, the first of his acts of long ago...." The passage is speaking of the figure of Wisdom, which provides the background for much of New Testament preexistence Christology (John 1, Col 1:15–20, etc.), but Christians in their devotional meditation and reflection have often applied it to Mary. Macquarrie is careful to point out, "The words, when applied to Mary, are not intended to suggest any pre-existence. But her ultimate or metaphysical conception had taken place in the beginning in the salvific purposes of God....He purposed to bring the human race not only into existence but into loving communion with himself."[10] It is something of a paradox, yet without impugning Mary's personal freedom to cooperate with God's salvific plan for humankind, Mary's conception can hardly have been an "afterthought" for God, any more than the incarnation could have been.

Second, Mary's conception in the people of Israel: "No individual exists in a vacuum, but always in a stream of history and in a culture....For Mary this background was Israel.... Mary was that moment when the preparation was complete, conceived and brought forth as the culmination of a long history of education in the ways of God and a long expectation of a visitation from God."[11] God's long pedagogy of Israel, the chosen people, was marked by hopes and aspirations, stellar moments of response to God's grace and initiative, recorded in the experience of the people of Israel and inscribed in the texts of the Old Testament. Mary's coming to be is the climax of God's pedagogy.

Third, Mary's conception in the marriage relationship of her parents, Joachim and Anna, the names given to Mary's parents in the second-century text, the *Protoevangelium of James*. Even if these are not the actual names of her parents because they are shrouded in the mists of history and there is finally no way to know with certainty, Mary had parents, and further, had parents who loved her and brought her up exemplifying a remarkable degree of openness to the God of Israel. John Macquarrie writes, "If we could imagine a child conceived out of pure love before God, would not such a child from the very moment of conception—I mean, conceived in the loving desire of the parents for the child even before they came together in sexual union—would not such a child be from the beginning the recipient of grace?"[12] Thus, the notion of conception in the immaculate conception already can be seen to have profound theological significance, a significance that is entirely appropriate across the spectrum of the Christian theological traditions.

Now we turn to the other term, *immaculate*. *Immaculate* introduces the issue of sin, *immaculate* meaning "unspotted." Our immediate problem is that we think of sin in an almost physical fashion, as an entity, as a stain. This is helpful in pointing up the disfigurement that sin brings about in the human person. Sin is a stain in the beauty, the holism, the possible perfection of the human person. However, while that is true, it is more fruitful to think of sin in personal and social terms. This would involve thinking of sin as "separation" or "alienation" or "estrangement," from God, and also from other people, and from the individual self. Such separation, estrangement, and alienation, because we are inextricably social persons and our personhood is constituted through relationality, demands an acknowledgment that the sin of one affects others, and the sin of one generation affects other generations yet to come. As Macquarrie has said, "No realistic theologian denies the fact that there is a human solidarity in sin and that this persists from generation to generation."[13] This approach to sin opens us up to a perhaps better understanding of what is meant by original sin. Original sin is the cumulative impact of the consequences of human sin—separation, estrangement, and alienation—for each and every generation.

"If such alienation characterizes the several dimensions of human life, we can see how it perpetuates itself from generation to generation and weighs upon every individual human life. This pervading alienation is original sin, but we see that it is nothing positive in itself. It is fundamentally a lack, the lack of a right relatedness."[14]

Now when it comes to speaking of our Lady, we can begin to see what *immaculate* might mean. *Immaculate* is not something negative, but positive. "When it is claimed that Mary was conceived free from original sin, what is meant is something affirmative. We are saying that she did not lack a right relationship with God....Alienation has been overcome or has never obtained, the channels from God are open, the moment is ripe for incarnation."[15] In this fundamental sense, the immaculate conception of our Blessed Lady becomes almost a corollary of the incarnation. If the moment is ripe for incarnation, then the fullness of the moment is ripe for incarnation, and not just the point of chronological time when Mary conceived the Son of God. The moment of her life, beginning with her conception, becomes part of that moment too. The immaculate conception is not only mariological but christological.

The immaculate conception is not only mariological and christological but also anthropological, that is, it has to do with what it means to be human. Continuing with this affirmative theology, Mary in the immaculate conception becomes the prototype of all humanity redeemed from original sin. Theologian Anthony Tambasco describes nicely this anthropological dimension of the immaculate conception: "Mary is from the first moment of her existence what we hope to become, at least by the final moment of our human pilgrimage....Original sin shows an unfaithful world. The Immaculate Conception shows that even the accumulated sinfulness of the world cannot overcome God's desire to save. It reveals the beginning of a new creation and the worth of the human person. What God did in Mary offers promise to the Church, and to each member."[16] The reality of our Lady's immaculate conception becomes the hope for all of us as it were.

THE ASSUMPTION OF MARY INTO HEAVEN

The assumption into heaven shows Mary as "the perfect type of the church," taken up by Christ to share his heavenly existence.[17] Macquarrie indicates that the assumption of Mary is dependent upon the ascension of Christ, and not simply its parallel: "The assumption of the blessed Virgin is dependent upon the ascension of Jesus Christ; it is indeed a corollary of it because of the glorification of human nature in him."[18] Or, according to Karl Rahner, SJ, "The [ascended Jesus Christ] did not go to a ready-made heaven that was awaiting him, rather he created heaven, understood as a nexus of personal relations."[19] Primary place in this heaven belongs to the woman whose assent became the vehicle for the consummation of God's graceful plan for humankind. The assumption is the transformation of Mary from her familiar earthly state to a new mode of being in which she enjoys a perfected and immediate relation to God. Since that perfected state is the hope of all Christians, what Mary enjoys through the assumption is the hope for each and every Christian: "It is not just a personal dogma about Mary (though it is that) but a dogma about the church, the whole body of the faithful of whom Mary is the type. Mary's glorious assumption, we may say, is the first moment in the glorious assumption of the church."[20] The same heavenly glory that she enjoys now, we also hope for. These approaches to the dogma of the assumption are particularly helpful. They help further to locate Mary within the horizon of experience of ordinary Christians, what we have called earlier in this book the "ecclesiotypical" approach to Mary. Where she has gone, we hope to follow.

In a recent popular book on Mary, the Irish Jesuit philosopher Thomas Casey takes this understanding a step further. He writes,

> The dogma of the Assumption is a dogma about one of the biggest issues anyone has to face: the value of human life. Do human beings have value? Are their lives worth living? Does everything end with death? And if not, what is there after death? The dogma was proclaimed in 1950, five years after the value of human life was shaken by some of the most horrific questions ever raised. World War II, the deadliest war in history, ended in 1945, with the estimated deaths of up to eighty-five million people. Among the victims were six million Jews, many of whom died in atrocious circumstances, after terrible abuse and torture. The dogma of the Assumption is a teaching about a Jewish woman, Mary of Nazareth. This fact is hugely significant in the context of the annihilation of millions of Jewish lives before and during the Second World War.[21]

At the very least, Casey is implicitly asking an important question. While it is true that the assumption of Mary is about the ultimate hope of all Christians, may it not feature also in a similar way for our Jewish brothers and sisters? This is not to impose, as it were, Catholic Marian doctrine and devotion on Judaism, but rather to recognize in a very fundamental way the fact that Mary was a Jewish woman. Perhaps the assumption of this very ordinary Jewish woman may help to build, in

The Marian Dogmas

however limited a fashion, bridges between Christianity and its mother faith.

CONCLUSION

Thinking about the two Marian dogmas of the immaculate conception and the assumption as they have been approached in this chapter seems to me to have two major values. First, we are enabled to see these dogmas as having to do not only with our Lady but also with ourselves. She is one of us. She is the first of the disciples of her Son and Lord. Second, a genuine contribution is made to the cause of Christian unity. Some of the concerns of Christians in the Reformed traditions about Mary are addressed and clarified. This does not mean that all the issues concerning Mary have gone away, but ecumenical baby steps have been taken, and that is no small thing.

11
AT THE SCHOOL OF MARY, "WOMAN OF THE EUCHARIST"

We simply do not know if Mary the mother of Jesus was present at the Last Supper or not. One could mount various kinds of arguments for and against her presence, but all such arguments are speculative. What is not speculative and what is not in question in Christian faith is Mary's presence in the Communion of Saints at every celebration of the Eucharist. She is the "woman of the Eucharist."

The personal devotion of Pope St. John Paul II to the blessed Virgin May is well known. The final chapter of Pope John Paul II's 2003 encyclical, *Ecclesia de Eucharistia* (Church from the Eucharist), is entitled "At the School of Mary, 'Woman of the Eucharist,'" and begins with these words: "If we wish to rediscover in all its richness the profound relationship between the Church and the Eucharist, we cannot neglect Mary, Mother and model of the Church....Mary can guide us toward this

At the School of Mary, "Woman of the Eucharist"

holy sacrament, because she herself has a profound relationship with it" (no. 53).[1]

Theologian Aidan Nichols, OP, has made the following comment apropos of this final section of the encyclical: "The Pope writes an entire 'Eucharistic Mariology' in small compass....It is a chapter future Church historians will note as marking the end of the reign of a low Mariology in modern Catholicism. It is also the most theologically original contribution the letter contains."[2] Much depends, of course, on what Nichols means by a "low Mariology." If he refers to efforts to retrieve something of the historical Mary, difficult though that project is due to the dearth of direct sources and data, then there has been not so much a "reign of low Mariology" as a rediscovery of the historical Mary. This rediscovery focuses on her Jewish background and culture, as historians and theologians seek to better understand the milieu of Second Temple Judaism in first-century Galilee. This scholarly work is surely valuable and does not merit the pejorative description of a "low Mariology." If, however, Nichols is describing what one contemporary author has titled "Missing Mary," that is, the somewhat diminished place of Mariology in the postconciliar Church, then *Ecclesia de Eucharistia* certainly places our Lady in a central theological position, and a central theological position vis-à-vis the Eucharist.[3]

While the Gospels are utterly silent about the presence of Mary at the Last Supper, the Acts of the Apostles affirms her presence with the early Christian community, at Pentecost (Acts 1:14). The Holy Father infers that Mary must have been present too at the first Christians' "breaking of the bread" (Acts 2:42). While we cannot be sure about that historically, what is clear, however, is that Mary may be described as "a 'woman of the Eucharist' in her whole life" (*Ecclesia de Eucharistia* 53).

MARY IN THE CHRISTIAN TRADITION

THE ANNUNCIATION

There is a fundamental sense in which the incarnation was dependent upon our Lady's decision. In Greek mythology the god Zeus seduces the goddess Europa. There is no seduction in Christianity. Mary was free to choose to be *Theotokos*, the God-bearer, or not. Catholic theologian Tina Beattie has captured the scene of the annunciation finely in these words: "Christianity originates in a story of mutual loving endeavour between a woman and God....God waited while Mary deliberated. The history of the world hung in the balance as a young girl considered the options before her. Then she said, 'I am the handmaid of the Lord, let what you have said be done to me.' And she stepped into the whirlwind."[4] Beattie's statement helps us to understand that our Lady did not have an infallibly clear understanding of the mystery of the incarnation, as a result of the annunciation. Rather, she stepped into the whirlwind that marks all human parenting, and a fortiori the parenting of our Lord Jesus Christ.

Of course, theologians are not the only commentators and interpreters of the annunciation. The annunciation of the angel Gabriel to our Blessed Lady has always had an enormous attraction for artists and poets. One thinks, for example, of Duccio's *Maesta* in Siena. Duccio (ca. 1255–1318) is regarded as one of the finest Italian artists of the Middle Ages. In this particular painting, as Gabriel greets Mary, the index finger of her right hand is pointing away from her toward her right. Originally, Mary was pointing to the vast main panel of the painting, which shows our Lady and the Christ-Child enthroned with all the angels, and also with saints from different centuries.[5] The message is clear. The incarnation-from-annunciation is at the heart of heaven, the heart of the Communion of Saints.

Mary's eucharistic faith emerges in the incarnation as she opens herself to receive the Word of God. Pope St. John

At the School of Mary, "Woman of the Eucharist"

Paul II writes, "At the Annunciation Mary conceived the Son of God in the physical reality of his body and blood, thus anticipating within herself what to some degree happens sacramentally in every believer who receives, under the signs of bread and wine, the Lord's body and blood" (*Ecclesia de Eucharistia* 55). There are two related dimensions of eucharistic meaning to this biblical scene, the ecclesial and the personal. After his initial greeting and our Lady's discomfort, the angel Gabriel then says to Mary words that are truly significant: "Do not be afraid!" (Luke 1:30). The angel speaks those words to us also: "Do not be afraid!" We are so often ruled by fear, and fear cripples us. It drains our energy and freezes us into immobility: fear of others, fear of not looking good in the eyes of others, fear of taking informed and significant decisions for ourselves, even fear of God. The angel tells Mary and tells all of us to let go of that debilitating fear—"Cast it out!"

At the ecclesial level, Mary's *Fiat* initiates her motherhood of the Church. "The Yes of Mary opens for [God] the place where he can pitch his tent. She herself becomes a tent for him, and thus she is the beginning of the Holy Church, which in her turn points forward to the New Jerusalem, in which there is no temple any more, because God himself dwells in her midst."[6] There is a direct line, as it were, from the annunciation to the Cross—to the gift of the dying Christ of his mother to every beloved disciple—and on to the Parousia where the sacramentality of the Church is no longer necessary. At the more personal level, the annunciation scene leads the Holy Father to posit "a profound analogy between the *Fiat* which Mary said in reply to the angel, and the *Amen* which every believer says when receiving the body of the Lord" (*Ecclesia de Eucharistia* 55).

To aid our understanding of the eucharistic dimension of the annunciation scene, we might draw upon a poem by the Scottish poet Edwin Muir (1887–1959). Edwin Muir is not well known in the United States, so a word of introduction may be in order. He was born and brought up in the Orkney Islands. His family moved to the slums of Glasgow, the industrial heartland of Scotland. This was a shattering experience for Muir. In his diary for 1939, he wrote,

> Once long ago when I was sitting in a crowded tramcar in Glasgow, I was overcome by the feeling that all the people there were animals; a collection of animals all being borne along in a curious contrivance in a huge city where, far and wide, there was not an immortal soul. I did not believe in immortality at the time, and thought I was happy in my unbelief....But now I know that if you deny people immortality you deny them humanity.[7]

For Muir there was a long and painful process of rediscovery, what might be called a conversion experience. He resented the impact that a certain harsh version of Calvinism had on Scottish life and culture. He speaks of "King Calvin" with his "iron pen" and "angry God."[8] Whether Muir is being fair to Calvin is not the issue here. The issue is that he is describing his experience of an imposed Calvinist ethos and culture, and he finds this ideological, lacking in humanity, lacking in life. He turns to a softer and more humane Mediterranean ethos and culture. During travels in Italy, he was struck by an image of the annunciation:

> I remember stopping for a long time one day to look at a little plaque in the wall of a house in the Via degli Artisti, representing the Annunciation. An angel and a young girl, their bodies inclined towards each other, their knees bent as if they were overcome by love, *'tutto tremante,'* gazed upon each

other like Dante's pair; and that representation of a human love so intense that it could not reach further, seemed the perfect earthly symbol of the love that passes understanding.[9]

The impact of this image and further meditation on it led to his wonderful poem, "The Annunciation." In this poem Muir describes the angel Gabriel addressing Mary (as in Luke 2) until each one reflects the other's face; that is to say, until Mary reflects heaven's message of the incarnation and Gabriel reflects Mary's willing and obedient response.

Muir was not a theologian but his "The Annunciation" is profoundly theological and, I would claim, eucharistic. God's messenger, the angel Gabriel looks into Mary's face with his message. What is his message? The Word of God is waiting to be enfleshed within her. The gaze, then, will continue, eyes meeting eyes, until Mary's consent shines in his eyes, and the Word shines in her womb, till "heaven in hers, and earth in his shine steady." Isn't this what the Eucharist is all about? Christ's gift-gaze meets ours till his heaven becomes ours, and our earth becomes his.

> Mary has literally allowed something—someone—beyond herself, beyond her furthest imagining—to come to life in her....She is still emphatically the human woman Mary; but she is also the one in whom the presence of God is growing moment by moment in the long, mysterious and subtle process of pregnancy....God's everlasting gift of himself that is the Son, the Word, emerges from her to begin that life which will change everything in creation. But we are called to the same job, to give God room so that we may be changed, so that the eternal Word will live in us and speak and act in love to others.[10]

At the center of this lies the Eucharist just as at Mary's center lay the embryonic Christ. Or, returning to Duccio, our eucharistic incarnation in Christ and his in us, enables us, like our Lady, to point to our enthronement by God's grace in the company of heaven, surrounded by the angels and the saints.

There is an urgency to our eucharistic appropriation of the annunciation. It is finely captured in a wonderful passage from one of St. Bernard of Clairvaux's sermons. Bernard acknowledges that God is waiting for Mary's reply, and in quite a daring way writes, "Why are you hesitating? Why are you fearful?...Behold, the One for whom all peoples are longing stands without and knocks on the door. Ah, what if he were to pass on because you hesitated...get up, run, open up!"[11] These last three verbs of Bernard's have a sense of urgency finely conveyed in the crisp imperative of the Latin: *Surge, curre, aperi!* As we make the scene part of our own faith and eucharistic practice, the imperative is issued to each of us: "Get up, run, open up!"

THE VISITATION

Continuing with the encyclical we read, "When at the Visitation, she bore in her womb the Word made flesh, she became in some way a 'tabernacle'—the first 'tabernacle' in history—in which the Son of God, still invisible to our human gaze, allowed himself to be adored by Elizabeth, radiating his light as it were through the eyes and the voice of Mary" (no. 55). The secret of the spiritual interpretation of the episode of the visitation lies in 2 Samuel 6. The ark of the covenant is being brought by King David into the city of Jerusalem. David exclaims, "How can the ark of the LORD come into my care?" (2 Sam 6:9). So he diverted the ark to the house of Obed-edom. After three months, during which God blesses Obed-edom,

At the School of Mary, "Woman of the Eucharist"

David finally receives the ark, leaping and dancing for joy before it, just as John the Baptist in Elizabeth's womb leaps and dances for joy before the new ark that is Mary.[12] We too are Mary in holy communion as we become arks of God's covenanting presence.

THE PRESENTATION OF THE CHILD JESUS IN THE TEMPLE

"Mary, throughout her life at Christ's side and not only on Calvary, made her own the sacrificial dimension of the Eucharist" (*Ecclesia de Eucharistia* 56). In this context, the Holy Father points to the episode of the presentation of Jesus in the Jerusalem temple (Luke 2:22). Simeon's words to Mary, "A sword will pierce your own soul too" (Luke 2:35).

The pope writes, "Mary experienced a kind of 'anticipated Eucharist'—one might say a 'spiritual communion'—of desire and of oblation, which would culminate in her union with her Son in his passion, and then find expression after Easter by her partaking in the Eucharist which the apostles celebrated as the memorial of that passion" (no. 56). May we not, as Mary, conjoin eucharistically the many swords that pierce our souls as we make our pilgrim way through life?

MOTHER OF THE CHURCH

On the cross in St. John's Gospel, Christ gave his mother to the beloved disciple and the beloved disciple to his mother (John 19:26–27). Mary is the "Mother of the Church." When our Lord entrusted his mother to the beloved disciple, it is interesting that St. John did not, in fact nowhere records explicitly his name. At the foot of the cross the reason for this anonymity may be provided. In giving Mary to the beloved disciple, our Blessed Lord is giving her to each of us as our mother. We are all disciples beloved of our Lord, and, therefore, with Mary for mother. It follows then, in the words of the pope: "Mary is present, with the Church and as the Mother of the Church, at each of our celebrations of the Eucharist. If the Church and the Eucharist are inseparably united, the same ought to be said of Mary and the Eucharist" (no. 57).

THE EUCHARISTIC MAGNIFICAT

Pope John Paul II continues in his reflection with these words: "In the Eucharist the Church is completely united to Christ and his sacrifice, and makes her own the spirit of Mary. This truth can be understood more deeply by *re-reading the Magnificat* in a Eucharistic key" (no. 58). To appreciate more fully the Holy Father's meaning let us recall the actual words of the Magnificat (Luke 1:46–55):

> My soul magnifies the Lord,
>> and my spirit rejoices in God my Savior,
> for he has looked with favor upon the lowliness of
>> his servant.
>> Surely, from now on all generations will call me blessed;
> for the Mighty One has done great things for me,
>> and holy is his name.
> His mercy is for those who fear him
>> from generation to generation.
> He has shown strength with his arm;
>> he has scattered the proud in the thoughts of their hearts.
> He has brought down the powerful from their thrones,
>> and lifted up the lowly;
> he has filled the hungry with good things,
>> and sent the rich away empty.

At the School of Mary, "Woman of the Eucharist"

> He has helped his servant Israel,
>   in remembrance of his mercy,
> according to the promise he made to our ancestors,
>   to Abraham and to his descendants forever.

What would that rereading of the Magnificat in a eucharistic key look like? It comes to expression in three formal, fundamental ways:

1. *In praise and thanksgiving.* Mary praises God "through" Jesus, but also "in" him and "with" him. "This is itself the true 'Eucharistic attitude'" (*Ecclesia de Eucharistia* 58). When we really praise someone, "we step back, we put our own preoccupations and goals and plans aside so as to let the reality of something else live in us for that moment, find room in us. Real praise is about forgetting myself, even my feelings, so that the sheer beauty and radiance of something beyond myself comes alive in me."[13] Praise is the opposite of egocentrism and the constant tendency toward narcissism.
2. *In recalling the wonders of salvation history.* God's wondrous working in Israel in the past comes in Christian understanding to climax in the wonder of the incarnation (cf. Luke 1:55). God's presence to Israel and in Israel becomes, as it were, God's presence as an Israelite.
3. *In reflecting the eschatological tension of the Eucharist.* When Christ comes to us in the "poverty" of the sacramental signs of bread and wine, the new heavens and the new earth are seminally present, calling into judgment the power structures of this earth, and inviting all to fuller life. That fuller life anticipates its plenary presence in the Parousia. The Eucharist anticipates sacramentally the Parousia.

Though the pope does not do this as such in his encyclical letter, we may see the very words of the Magnificat addressed to each communicant within a eucharistic ecology. Let us develop this eucharistic ecology with reference to the verses of the hymn. In verses 46–47 Mary's posture is ours at holy communion as we praise God our Savior for having regarded our lowliness: "Lord, I am not worthy that you should enter under my roof, but only say the word and my soul shall be healed." Similarly, in verse 52 we recognize that there are in Christ no mighty ones on their thrones. We are all of low degree but raised high in receiving him. Truly, as in verse 53 he has filled us with good things, with himself, that than which nothing better can be received. The pope concludes this final section of his encyclical: "The Eucharist has been given to us so that our life, like that of Mary, may become completely a *Magnificat!*" (no. 58).

CONCLUSION: AN ECUMENICAL HOPE

The respected Lutheran theologian George Lindbeck says of this chapter on Mary in the encyclical,: "Marian devotion is now alien to Protestant, including Lutheran, sensibilities, but Brother Martin (and *a fortiori*, the Augsburg Confession) would have no objections to the form that it here takes. Indeed, one can easily imagine Luther making his own the chapter's concluding sentences."[14] Not all Christians, needless to say, will identify with the sentiments of George Lindbeck. Our Blessed Lady remains a problem for many of our sisters and brothers in the Reformation traditions, although as this book has been suggesting, this has been changing through greater ecumenical understanding. Nonetheless, as our Lady is theologically and devotionally more closely aligned with

At the School of Mary, "Woman of the Eucharist"

the *Ecclesia de Eucharistia*, the "Church from the Eucharist," perhaps her role will become less divisive ecumenically and more unitive. Perhaps. But at least, as Catholics study and further their appreciation of Pope John Paul's "At the School of Mary," in his *Ecclesia de Eucharistia*, the low Mariology remarked on by Aidan Nichols, OP, at the outset of our reflection may really come to an end, and a more integral ecclesial and indeed eucharistic Mariology will emerge.

12
PRAYING THE ROSARY

> At its simplest and most obvious, the figure of the Madonna cradling her child on her breast has placed at the center of our experience of the grace of God an unforgettable image of human tenderness and nurture. In its light, the cross is more readily understood as an act of love.
>
> Eamon Duffy[1]

For countless Catholics, daily praying has taken the familiar shape of the Rosary. The period 1830–1960 was one of intense mariological discussion and fervent Marian devotion. Yet it seems that devotion to Mary has too often in the years after Vatican II ceased to be a vibrant part of Catholic life, something that will be considered later in chapter 13. Nonetheless, it is my profound conviction that Marian devotion will not simply disappear. Is this just whistling in the dark? I do not think so. Consider, for example, this persuasive passage from Andrew Greeley, the priest-storyteller-sociologist:

> Catholics live in an enchanted world, a world of statues and holy water, stained-glass and votive

candles, saints and religious medals, rosary beads and holy pictures. But these Catholic paraphernalia are mere hints of a deeper and more pervasive religious sensibility which inclines Catholics to see the Holy lurking in creation. As Catholics, we find our houses and our world haunted by a sense that the objects, events, and persons of daily life are revelations of grace.

This is the Catholic sacramental imagination, or more technically analogical imagination. It will not go away, but it will develop. Greeley puts it superbly and with a sense of humor when he continues:

> If the high tradition is to be found in theology books and the documents of the councils, and the papacy, and various hierarchies of the world, popular tradition is to be found in the rituals, the art, the music, the architecture, the devotions, the stories of ordinary people. If the former can be stated concisely at any given time in creeds which are collections of prose propositions, the latter is fluidly, amorphously, and elusively expressed in stories. Prosaic people that we are, we members of the Catholic elite are inclined to believe that the real Catholicism is that of the high tradition. Doctrine and dogma are more important than experience and narrative....The Christmas crib is popular Catholicism; the decrees of Chalcedon are high Catholicism. The same story of God among us is told by both, the same fundamental reality of our faith is disclosed by both, the same rumor of angels is heard in both. Which, however, has more impact on the lives of ordinary Catholics? Anyone who thinks that homoousios is

more important to ordinary folk than the Madonna and her Child is incurably prosaic—besides being wrong!"[2]

As a theologian who writes prose and runs the risk of being prosaic, I cannot go all the way with Greeley. Both the high tradition and the popular tradition are equally important. Indeed, it may even be that they act as mutual correctives to one another. Greeley, however, is surely right in implying that if the Christmas crib represents popular Christology, the Rosary represents popular Mariology.

THE ROSARY AND THE CATHOLIC IMAGINATION

Add to Fr. Greeley's perspective the following comment from a philosopher: "Icons are filled with the reality to which they refer because the reality expresses itself in the icon. Anybody kissing an icon touches Christ and, kissing, receives his grace. Children already know this when they will not sleep without their comfort blanket."[3] Kissing an icon is touching Christ and his grace. Praying the Rosary is touching Mary, who is most profoundly and uniquely in touch with Christ and his grace. This makes so much sense to me. Catholicism is known as the Christian tradition that is multisensory in its expression and in its experience of God. Catholics like smells and bells! We use incense, we use bells, our olfactory sense and our auditory sense. We use holy pictures, we use bright colors, we use art, our visual sense. We like to touch holy things, like statues, like rosary beads—and so our tactile sense is in touch with the experience of God.

Some people might take issue with the philosopher's likening of icons, such as rosary beads with a comfort blanket. I do not think this necessarily takes us to the psychotherapist for help. It's just nice to *feel* the divine, to be "in touch" with God. Matter mediates God and the things of God for Catholics. I like to sleep with my rosary beads under my pillow. What is it about the telling of beads with one's fingers as one prays the Rosary? I think part of the answer lies in this need to touch God as it were, to touch our Lady. We have an instinctive human need to reach out and actually catch the divine. Maybe a couple of examples will help. There is a large statue of St. Peter in St. Peter's Basilica in Rome, and the feet are worn down by pilgrims over many centuries touching and kissing the feet of the statue. This is an expression of the need to touch God, to touch the things of God. Take another example, that of icons. Christians think of icons as windows into the divine, windows, if you will, into the heart of God, into the heart of heaven. This certainly seems to be how Orthodox Christians experience icons. Orthodox Christians love to touch icons, to kiss icons, and I imagine this touching and kissing of icons brings them to an awareness, a tactile awareness of the holy presence of God.

THE ROSARY IS THEOCENTRIC AND CHRISTOCENTRIC

The very shape of the prayers in the Rosary, although it is a Marian devotion, is God-centered. Think of how we say the prayers: the Lord's Prayer, the Hail Mary, and the Gloria. The Lord's Prayer is given to us by the Lord Jesus, God in the flesh. We address God in the words he gave to us. Then the Hail Mary, the first part of which is just the words of Holy Scripture in the Gospel of St. Luke, chapters 1—2. The second part of the Hail Mary comes from a Dominican in the fifteenth century. "In the fifteenth century...Peter

Nigri (d. 1483), composed the second half of the Ave prayer. This addition to the scriptural words addressed to Mary naturally assumes that Mary has an active role interceding for the Church militant and its people. It encouraged having recourse to Mary as an ally in the invocation of Christ and of God."[4] Then, having acknowledged the place of Mary in the history of salvation, having acknowledged her place as first in the Communion of Saints, we returned with the Gloria to the God with whom we began, only this time in an expressly trinitarian fashion. So, those who think that this prayer of the Rosary is exclusively Marian could not be further from the truth. This same point is made very well by Pope St. John Paul II in his encyclical letter on the Rosary:

> The rosary, though clearly Marian in *character, is at heart a Christocentric prayer. In the sobriety of its elements, it has all the depth of* the gospel message in its entirety, of which it can be said to be a compendium....At the most superficial level, the beads often become a simple counting mechanism to mark the succession of Hail Marys. Yet they can also take on a symbolism which can give added depth to contemplation. Here the first thing to note is the way the beads converge upon the crucifix. Which both opens and closes the unfolding sequence of prayer. The life and prayer of believers is centered upon Christ. Everything begins from him, everything leads toward him, everything, through him, in the Holy Spirit, attains to the Father.[5]

The Rosary is both theocentric and christocentric. It should also be noted, moreover, that a growing number of our sisters and brothers in the Reformation tradition are discovering the biblical foundation and orientation of the Rosary.

Praying the Rosary

MARY AND THE CHRISTIAN PRAYING THE ROSARY

Pope St. John Paul II has written, "It can be said that the rosary is, in some sense, a prayer-commentary on the final chapter of the Vatican II Constitution *Lumen Gentium*, a chapter which discusses the wondrous presence of the Mother of God in the mystery of Christ and the church."[6] This, of course, reflects the conciliar approach to our Lady, situating her ecclesiologically, something discussed earlier in chapter 11—Mary is both Mother of the Church, in the proclamation of Pope Paul VI, and the first in the community of disciples. However, if the Rosary and Marian devotion are to be recommended to modern Catholics and indeed other Christians, then the ecclesiological situating of Mary must be more practically grounded. The challenge: How is that to be done?

Perhaps a start can be made with some words of Timothy Radcliffe, OP: "The mysteries of the rosary have been compared with the *Summa Theologiae* of St. Thomas. They tell, in their own way, of how everything comes from God, and everything returns to God."[7] If the mysteries are, therefore, theocentric and christocentric, portraying how everything originates in God and finds its *telos* in God, then, the mysteries tell of how *I* come from God and return to God. The Rosary is the proclamation of the "good news" in the entire event of Jesus, and equally is the proclamation of "good news" to the individual person, to everyone. What Radcliffe implies in practical terms is this: what is said of Mary may be said appropriately of the Church, that is to say, of you and of me. Let us explore this through some of the mysteries. From the joyful mysteries, first, the enunciation of the angel Gabriel to Mary. I teach in a building at Mount Angel Seminary called "Annunciation." You can see how appropriate this is for the business of doing theology, and not only with seminarians.

MARY IN THE CHRISTIAN TRADITION

The angel Gabriel brought the good news by invitation to Mary that she was to become pregnant with God. In learning theology, and teaching theology, we are about the business of becoming pregnant with God, as it were. What is said of Mary in this event of the annunciation is said of us, appropriately and with qualification. *We* are "full of grace," in the sense that the "Lord is with us." Through the Holy Spirit we are brought forth as daughters/sons in the Son. We put ourselves at God's service, "Behold, we are the handmaids of the Lord...."

According to Elaine Park, the narrative is patterned after the story in 2 Samuel 6, the story of King David dancing before the ark of the covenant. We may see Mary as the new ark of the covenant, with John the Baptist "dancing" in Elizabeth's womb. Mary is a believer in Elizabeth's words, "Blessed is she who believed..." (Luke 1:45). As Scripture scholar Elaine Park has said, "Mary is placed centrally among all those who believe; she presents a model for believers and becomes an image of the church."[8] Then Mary proclaims the Magnificat. We are arks of the covenant, bearing the Christ presence within us. We are believers. We proclaim the Magnificat too: "When something is magnified, what is already there becomes more evident; it is enlarged for those who would not otherwise see all the details....Mary [and we] magnifies, heightens, amplifies the image of God in such a way that those of us who are nearsighted or myopic can see more clearly who God is and how God acts."[9]

The third joyful mystery is the nativity of Jesus. In St. Luke's infancy narrative, Jesus is the son of David, the Savior, born in Bethlehem, and his birth is announced to the shepherds. In St. Matthew's infancy narrative, Jesus is God-with-as, Emmanuel. The third joyful mystery is about God coming to birth in our midst. It is about the incarnation. How, we may ask, is the incarnation about us? It is put best by Meister Eckhart, the medieval Dominican mystic, who makes the

Praying the Rosary

point that there is no point to the incarnation unless Christ is coming to incarnation in us.[10]

The sorrowful mysteries of the Rosary almost need no comment in this regard: the agony in the garden of Gethsemane, the scourging at the pillar, the crowning with thorns, the carrying of the cross, the crucifixion and death of Jesus. Each of them deals with the pain and suffering of Jesus in the last twenty-four hours of his earthly life. It hardly needs to be pointed out that each one of them speaks to our human predicament also. There are times when we are in agony in our own Gethsemane. There are times when we feel scourged at the pillar of life. There is no one who is not crowned with thorns at some time in life. And carrying the cross? We all have crosses to carry. You do not need to look for a cross to carry; the cross of suffering will find you. And then there is the agony of death. Irish novelist and writer Nuala O'Faolain, in her autobiographical memoir, wrote the following about Good Friday, as she wandered into the pro-Cathedral in Dublin: "[I saw] the purple cloths they cover the images with, during Holy Week, to remind us of Christ's Passion. What about the ordinary passion of people! I thought. Look how much ordinary men and women know about being crucified! No wonder we strain ourselves to believe that there is a God, who loves us."[11] I find that a very sad comment because that is what Good Friday is about, about the crucifixion of ordinary people. Of course, Good Friday/God's Friday is about the historic crucifixion that happened once upon a time in Jerusalem, demonstrating uniquely the *telos* of God's love. But, since we are conjoined to Christ through baptism, Good Friday is about us conjoined with Christ. The sorrowful mysteries of the Rosary are not just about our Lord Jesus Christ on the day he died. They are also about our own sorrowful mysteries. Think of the marvelous words of the sixteenth-century mystic Benedict of Canfield (1563–1610), in his *Rule of Perfection*, 1609:

127

Therefore our own pains—insofar as they are not ours but those of Christ—must be deeply respected. How wonderful! And more: our pains are as much to be revered as those of Jesus Christ in his own passion. For if people correctly adore him with so much devotion in images on the Good Friday cross, why may we not then revere him on the living cross that we ourselves are?

If the sorrowful mysteries are all about our blessed Lord, the glorious mysteries are about the glorification of Jesus, and the glorification of Mary as first in the Communion of Saints. They are also about our glorification: the resurrection of Jesus, the ascension of Jesus, the descent of the Holy Spirit at Pentecost, the assumption of Mary into heaven, the coronation of Mary as queen of heaven. Let us take just a few examples from the glorious mysteries to see how they apply to us, and not simply to Jesus and Mary. The resurrection of Jesus is also about our resurrection. He is the first one of many brothers. He is the first fruits to be raised in the harvest of resurrection. We are the remaining harvest. Quite simply, there is no Christ without us. He wants us, and he wants us to be and to experience his finalization in resurrection. Or, consider the descent of the Holy Spirit at Pentecost. The Spirit did not come once only but the Spirit continues to come. The Spirit will always come. Cardinal Basil Hume, archbishop of Westminster, was fond of saying, "Pentecost is today, and every day. Pentecost is today, and always." This is true not just generically for the whole Church, but every day for you and me. When we pray this glorious mystery, we are reminding ourselves that today the Holy Spirit is coming to us. Pentecost is ours, today and every day!

What about the luminous mysteries, the mysteries created by Pope St. John Paul II? The luminous mysteries are,

Praying the Rosary

he says, "five significant moments—'luminous mysteries'—during this phase of Christ's life."[12] They are the following: the baptism of Jesus, the self-manifestation of Christ at the wedding at Cana, the proclamation of the kingdom of God, the transfiguration of Jesus, the institution of the Eucharist. You can probably see how this will go. Each one of these mysteries refers to a light-filled event in the life of the Lord. Just as equally, each one of the mysteries refers to the light-filled reality that God's grace makes of us, and the light-filled reality we are destined to become. The baptism of Jesus transforms Jesus from being an unknown nobody, as it were, you being a fearless preacher, one totally committed to the reality of his God, his Abba, his Father. Isn't that in a sense what baptism does for us? It transforms us from being unknown nobodies into the Body of Christ. We become the Body of Christ in and through baptism. Just as the baptism of Jesus issued in his public proclamation, so our baptism issues in our public proclamation, our public example of what it means to be the Body of Christ, our particular witness to Christian faith. Next, the institution of the Eucharist. I can think of many ways in which the Eucharist and its institution applies to us. Obviously, it was the most central event in the whole life of Jesus, on the night before he died. He gave himself away as our food and drink. One of the ways we can be eucharistic as Jesus is eucharistic is by giving ourselves away, even unto death. For example, living our marriage and our sexuality in the light of the Eucharist. Jesus's entire life was *the* manifestation of the God who is Love; he is about self-gift, and this is especially true of the Eucharist: "This is my body, this is my blood for you." Timothy Radcliffe makes the connection superbly:

> When Jesus hands over his body to the disciples he is vulnerable. He is in their hands for them to do as they wish. One has already sold him, another will

deny him, and most of the rest will run away. The gift of his body discloses that sexuality is inseparable from vulnerability. It embodies a tenderness which means that one may get hurt....The Last Supper shows us with extreme realism the perils of giving ourselves to anyone. It is not a romantic tryst in a candlelit trattoria....The Last Supper is the story of the risk of giving yourself to others.[13]

The marriage vows are explicitly eucharistic: "This is me for you, to death."

CONCLUSION

These few examples provide some indication of how praying the Rosary not only rehearses the central stories of our redemption, the central stories of Scripture with regard to Jesus and with regard to Mary, but also indicate simultaneously how the mysteries of the Rosary are our mysteries too. When we pray them, we are thinking. Praying is thinking! We are thinking not simply about Jesus, we are thinking not simply about Mary, but we are also thinking in a particularly intense way about who we are in Christ, about who we are as Christ's holy Body. We are praying our own mysteries.

13

MARY TODAY

> The Virgin Mary has touched more people than any other woman in history, and for many reasons.
>
> Thomas G. Casey, SJ[1]

> Mary cannot be rightly conformed to any stereotype, ancient or modern.
>
> John Macquarrie[2]

In a recent popular book on Mary, Irish Jesuit philosopher Thomas Casey makes a very interesting comment:

> Over the last sixty years or so, Catholics, at least in the Western world, have moved from a situation where Marian devotion was simply taken for granted to a new situation where it now demands a real effort to return to our Lady in any meaningful way. Nowadays, Catholics are more likely to carry iPods rather than rosary beads, and to sport a tattoo instead of wearing the miraculous medal. It's a sea-change, and yet it has happened without fanfare,

almost without noticing it, "off stage," as the late Irish poet Seamus Heaney would have put it.³

It is true that iPods and tattoos need little comment in our contemporary culture, but it might be helpful to situate the "off stage" comment of Seamus Heaney. It comes from a poem by Heaney with the title "Like Everybody Else" in which he describes his departure from regular eucharistic celebration. Heaney tells us in the poem that he had no big argument with himself, no great philosophical concerns over transubstantiation or anything like that. Rather, the departure happened "off stage," that is to say, in Thomas Casey's terms, "almost without noticing it." In all probability he gave up going regularly to Mass, and this became something of a habit, and so his appreciation of the Eucharist waned, although the poem intimates not completely. This seems to me a very good parallel for describing what happened to Marian devotion for Catholics in the post–Vatican II era. For all kinds of reasons it just waned, but we are the poorer for that waning.

There may, however, be a little more to it than Fr. Casey suggests. In his justly celebrated *Mary for All Christians*, theologian John Macquarrie has a concluding chapter entitled "Mary and Modernity."⁴ In this chapter he points out that contemporary Christians stand in two different worlds, as it were, the post-Enlightenment world beginning in the eighteenth century, and their received world of Christian faith. The former has given rise to the magnificent developments in science and technology, as well as giving emphasis to a critique of all received beliefs and values and most especially those of Christianity. Living in these two worlds can be somewhat uncomfortable because of the experienced tensions between them. "[Contemporary Christians] feel the continuing power of their Christian heritage, and they want to affirm it. But they want also to affirm the intellectual and political values that

Mary Today

emerged two or three hundred years ago," and Macquarrie concludes that "we have not yet found a satisfactory way of reconciling these conflicting loyalties."[5]

In respect of Mary and of devotion to her the Christian's dilemma is posed quite sharply: Is the contemporary Christian to maintain devotion to Mary with all of its multifaceted traditions, legends, devotional practices, and perhaps hyperbolic utterances flowing from the long Christian tradition? Or is the Christian of today, in order to be a modern person, to abandon all of this? Perhaps we could put it like this: Is the contemporary Christian to advocate an either-or approach or a both-and approach to Marian tradition?

Putting it like this, let us turn to some insights from church historian and theologian Eamon Duffy. "One of the most striking developments in post-conciliar Catholicism has been the way in which Marian piety has simply ceased to feature as a vital dimension of their faith for a growing number of people"—thus Eamon Duffy writing in 2004.[6] Duffy goes on to point out that our Blessed Lady has been central in Catholicism both East and West for at least 1,500 years and so much so "that some sort of living Mariology must be judged one of its essential features, and not a devotional optional extra."[7]

In Duffy's analysis various factors come into play in this reduction of Marian piety in contemporary Catholicism. First, as Catholics have become more and more aware of Sacred Scripture, they have come to recognize that Mary has a much lesser role in the Scriptures than in the accumulated piety of the following centuries. This has led to some uncertainty about our Blessed Lady. Second, there is "a problem for many modern Christians in handling the mythic and poetic aspects of the cult of Mary," and Duffy points to some of the strange titles given to our Lady in the Litany of Loretto, for example—Ark of the Covenant, Tower of Ivory, Tower of David, Mystical Rose, and so on. Looking back to the chapter dealing with the

Scriptures, modern Christians might be able to see Mary as the ark of the covenant in a new light, given the visitation episode in St. Luke's Gospel. But what of these other titles? What are modern Catholics to make of these? Third, there is the nexus of emotions around Mary with all kinds of assumptions about sex and gender—Mary is a mother but also a virgin, and a perpetual virgin at that. In the sexual mores and practices of the twenty-first century, this may seem particularly strange. Finally, there tended to be in traditional Marian piety a very strong, perhaps even extreme emotional contrast between Mary and the ordinary Christian. Duffy describes it like this:

> The sinner approaching Mary never did so as like approaching like, but always the prodigal creeping shame-faced to a long-suffering, saintly and neglected mother....The continual insistence in these [traditional Victorian] hymns on the contrast between the purity and beauty of Mary on the one hand, and the vileness and degradation of the sinner on the other (often more or less explicitly associated with sexuality, since the focus of Mary's spiritual beauty was her chastity) probably also fostered a sense of alienation from self, a damaging loss of the sense of one's human and Christian dignity and potential, which may at times have hampered true repentance.[8]

One of Duffy's concluding comments in his analysis of this Marian predicament among Catholics is particularly interesting. It takes on a more particular political dimension. This is how he puts it:

> But there was behind this whole Marian piety a profounder alienation, a sense that in the modern world

the Christian had no role except that of denunciation. These [traditional Victorian compositions] were hymns for people without votes, or for those who disapproved of the stakes in which votes might be used. And much Marian devotion has had a disturbingly anti-Democratic dimension to it....I am not of course suggesting that everyone with a devotion to Mary before 1960 (or since) was a fascist: but I do want to suggest that the conventional forms of Marian devotion—the rhetoric of the hymns and prayers addressed to her, the selection of her attributes and privileges which were singled out for attention, and the cult stories associated with her pilgrimages—were often pressed into service to endorse social and political attitudes, and modes of self-perception and self-evaluation, which now seen alien and distasteful to many Christians....But I have no doubt that (sometimes subliminal) discomfort with such attitudes is partly responsible for the widespread loss of confidence in traditional Mariology, and that any new and healthy Marian piety will need to reorientate itself in order to free itself from this particular cultural, political and psychological heritage.[9]

Duffy believes that the germ of this reorientation may be found in Vatican II's teaching on Mary. He has in mind here especially the ecclesiotypical approach to Mary. In the teaching of Vatican II, "[Mary's] excellences and privileges, like her assumption into heaven, were not alienating measures of her distance from us, but pledges of the dignity which awaits us all, and which, in grace, is already taking shape within us."[10] The approach advocated by Duffy has contemporary Christians standing firmly in both worlds, the world of Enlightenment modernity and the world of Christian tradition. The challenge is how to achieve this dual standing.

PRACTICAL SUGGESTIONS

"For many English-speaking Catholics before the Vatican Council, Marian piety was second only to Eucharistic devotion as the formative and most vital element in their personal spirituality."[11] Even as he analyzes some of the factors that make for our reduction in Marian piety today, Eamon Duffy laments the loss "of a vital dimension of poetry and tenderness" for Catholic spirituality.[12] It would be very hard to disagree with Duffy. Becoming a Catholic Christian or wishing to remain one is a matter of choice, a fairly clear but deliberate choice. There are so many choices a person can make about how to live in our complex but beautiful world, but choosing Catholicism seems to me one of the very best things one can do. Within that choice there are some nonnegotiables: growing awareness of Holy Scripture and doctrine; developing participation in the sacramental life of the Church, and most especially regular participation in the Eucharist; taking responsibility for conscientious decision-making within the rich moral tradition of the Church, including a commitment to social justice; a regular schedule of prayer; and, I would add, devotion to our Blessed Lady. Thus, the question I want to ask is fairly simple: "Realistically, what might I do to shape devotion to our Lady in this day and age?"

- Find out something about Mary from the Gospels first of all, and then perhaps also from the rich treasury of reflection and devotion in the Church. It is impossible to love that which we do not know, and so start with learning something about Mary. This includes learning to reflect on our Blessed Lady not only with the great thinkers of the premodern epoch, but also with modern and, therefore, more critical theological thinkers. One thinks, for example, of John Macquarrie's book *Mary for All Christians*. In a different vein there is Elizabeth Johnson's *Truly Our Sister*, reflecting both a liberation and a feminist perspective. Studies such as these help the modern Christian to stand in both worlds.

- Learn to pray with and to Mary within the Communion of Saints. While study remains important for genuine growth in faith, it is also important to recall that we are not Cartesian brains on sticks. I am struck by an important comment made by Herbert McCabe: "The tradition was handed down not as a piece of information but as a recognition, a growing and more and more liberated recognition, of our right to praise [Mary] beyond all other creatures, to say that she was as holy as a redeemed creature could be."[13] Practically speaking, one might begin with learning by heart that constant Catholic prayer, "Hail Mary, full of grace...." This prayer is central to the Rosary and is replete with scriptural allusions. Perhaps this is the place to say something about Mary's intercession. When all is said and done about this aspect of Marian piety, one of the fundamental points—perhaps *the* fundamental point here—is that in prayer to the saints

> [Catholics] are confessing their belief in the reality of the church as a community united across the divide of death by faith in the one God, sharing a common hope for the coming of his kingdom, and bearing one another's burden in love as they move in pilgrimage towards that kingdom....To ask Mary's prayers, therefore, is not merely to invoke her help, but symbolically to ask, and

confess our dependence upon, the prayers of the whole church, living and dead....Catholics believe that [Mary's] prayers are a more perfect expression of the Spirit's utterance, and therefore have a value greater than those of any other Christian. But in the end that is what they are: the prayers of a Christian.[14]

This splendid passage from Eamon Duffy should help to ease the difficulties that some Christians might experience in praying to Mary, or in asking for Mary's assistance. It is a fundamental recognition of our common humanity with Mary and of our common membership in the Church of God, the Body of Christ.

- Learn to pray the Rosary, the subject of chapter 12 in this book, including the five extra mysteries of Pope St. John Paul II. Developing a discipline or a regular schedule for prayer is essential, and so resolving to pray the section of the Rosary every day is a very good thing: the joyful mysteries, the luminous mysteries, the sorrowful mysteries, the glorious mysteries.
- Place some images of Mary in your home or living space—statues, icons, holy pictures. Catholicism is a multisensory tradition and so engaging our sight this way can only be helpful, and it is a very helpful aid in catechizing our younger people.
- Engage with the local parish community (or with some other ecclesial community organization) in Marian devotion—public prayer, pilgrimage, educational opportunities, and so on.

These few practical suggestions, it seems to me, help the modern Christian to stand in both the worlds referred to above—the world of post-Enlightenment modernity and the world of traditioned Christian faith. Personally, I cannot see how Marian devotion in some shape and form cannot but remain within the fabric of Christian faith and devotion. It is too firmly rooted to vanish altogether. If, on the other hand, it is to remain as a firm root within the lives of individual Christians, then some personal choices need to be made. The choices mentioned here are those that occur to me.

NOTES

PREFACE

1. Owen F. Cummings, "Understanding the Immaculate Conception," *The Furrow* 12 (1979): 767–71.

1. THE HISTORICAL MARY OF NAZARETH

1. Elizabeth A. Johnson, *Truly Our Sister: A Theology of Mary in the Communion of Saints* (London: Continuum, 2003), 139.
2. John A. McGuckin, *The Westminster Handbook of Patristic Theology* (Louisville, KY: Westminster John Knox Press, 2004), 349.
3. Chris Maunder, "Mary in the New Testament and Apocrypha," in *Mary: The Complete Resource*, ed. Sarah Jane Boss (New York: Oxford University Press, 2007), 14.
4. John L. McKenzie, "The Mother of Jesus in the New Testament," in *Mary in the Churches*, ed. Hans Küng and Jurgen Moltmann (New York: Herder and Herder, 1983), 9.
5. Amy-Jill Levine, *The Misunderstood Jew* (New York: HarperCollins, 2007), 7.

6. Jaroslav Pelikan, *Jesus through the Centuries* (New York: Yale University Press, 1985), 20.

7. Tai Ilan, "Women in Jewish Life and Law," in *The Cambridge History of Judaism*, ed. Steven T. Katz (Cambridge: Cambridge University Press, 2006), 4:628. I am grateful to my colleague Dr. Mark Nussberger for drawing my attention to this essay.

8. Rabbi Nicholas de Lange, "A Woman in Israel," in *Mary and the Churches*, ed. Alberic Stacpoole, OSB (Slough: St. Paul Publications, 1982), 192–201.

9. Jon D. Levenson, *The Love of God* (Princeton: Princeton University Press, 2016), 7.

10. de Lange, "A Woman in Israel," 197.

11. de Lange, "A Woman in Israel," 199.

12. Mishnah, *Sotah* 3.4.

13. Ilan, "Women in Jewish Life and Law," 631.

14. de Lange, "A Woman in Israel," 193ff.

15. Geza Vermes, "Miriam the Jewess," *The Way Supplement* 45 (1982): 56.

16. Johnson, *Truly Our Sister*, 194.

17. John P. Meier, *A Marginal Jew: Rethinking the Historical Jesus* (New York: Doubleday, 1991), 276–77.

18. Geza Vermes, *Jesus the Jew* (Philadelphia: Fortress Press, 1973), 21–22.

19. F. L. Filas, "Joseph, St.," in *New Catholic Encyclopedia*, 2nd ed., vol. 7 (Farmington Hills, MI: Gale Research, 2002), 1035.

20. P. D. James, *Death in Holy Orders* (New York: Ballantyne Books, 2001), 69–70.

21. Meier, *A Marginal Jew*, 324.

22. Meier, *A Marginal Jew*, 209.

23. Mishnah, *Sotah* 1.5.

24. Meier, *A Marginal Jew*, 317–18.

Notes

25. Owen F. Cummings, "The Real Mary of Nazareth," *The Priest* 48 (1992): 17.

2. IMAGES OF MARY IN THE NEW TESTAMENT

1. Raymond E. Brown, *Biblical Exegesis and Church Doctrine* (New York: Paulist Press, 1985), 100.
2. Geoffrey Preston, *Faces of the Church* (Grand Rapids, MI: Eerdmans, 1997), 256.
3. Tina Beattie, *Rediscovering Mary: Insights from the Gospels* (Liguori, MO: Triumph Books, 1995), 8.
4. Brown, *Biblical Exegesis*, 87.
5. Brown, *Biblical Exegesis*, 88.
6. Ben Witherington III, *Grace in Galatia: A Commentary on Paul's Letter to the Galatians* (Grand Rapids, MI: Eerdmans, 1998), 288.
7. Lawrence S. Cunningham, "Born of a Woman (Gal. 4:4): A Theological Meditation," in *Mary Mother of God*, ed. Carl E. Braaten and Robert W. Jenson (Grand Rapids, MI: Eerdmans, 2004), 40.
8. Donald Senior, "Gospel Portrait of Mary: Images and Symbols from the Synoptic Tradition," in *Mary, Woman of Nazareth*, ed. Doris Donnelly (New York: Paulist Press, 1989), 92.
9. John Macquarrie, *Mary for All Christians* (Grand Rapids, MI: Eerdmans, 1990), 33.
10. Eamon Duffy, *What Catholics Believe about Mary* (London: Catholic Truth Society, 1989), 5.
11. John P. Meier, "The Brothers and Sisters of Jesus in Ecumenical Perspective," *Catholic Biblical Quarterly* 54 (1992): 27.
12. Macquarrie, *Mary for All Christians*, 35.
13. Eugene LaVerdiere, *The Beginning of the Gospel* (Collegeville, MN: Liturgical Press, 1999), 108.

14. Vincent P. Branick, "Mary in the Christologies of the New Testament," *Marian Studies* 32 (1981): 29.

15. See Hans von Campenhausen, *The Virgin Birth in the Theology of the Ancient Church* (Eugene, OR: Wipf and Stock, 2011), 8–9. The original English publication was in 1954.

16. Beverly R. Gaventa, *Mary: Glimpses of the Mother of Jesus* (Columbia: University of South Carolina Press, 1995), 29–48.

17. Gaventa, *Mary: Glimpses of the Mother of Jesus*, 33.

18. Gaventa, *Mary: Glimpses of the Mother of Jesus*, 38–39.

19. Gaventa, *Mary: Glimpses of the Mother of Jesus*, 39.

20. Gaventa, *Mary: Glimpses of the Mother of Jesus*, 43.

21. Brown, *Biblical Exegesis*, 92.

22. Stephen J. Shoemaker, *Mary in Early Christian Faith and Devotion* (New Haven: Yale University Press, 2016), 35.

23. Senior, "Gospel Portrait of Mary," 94.

24. Ignace de la Potterie, *Mary in the Mystery of the Covenant* (New York: Alba House, 1992), 4.

25. For some fine comments on the Magnificat, see the Old Testament scholar and Hebraist Samuel Terrien, *The Magnificat: Musicians as Biblical Interpreters* (Mahwah, NJ: Paulist Press, 1995).

26. Beverly R. Gaventa, "Nothing Will Be Impossible with God: Mary as the Mother of Believers," in *Mary Mother of God*, ed. Carl E. Braaten and Robert W. Jenson (Grand Rapids, MI: Eerdmans, 2004), 24.

27. Gaventa, "Nothing Will Be Impossible," 25–26.

28. Beattie, *Rediscovering Mary*, 21, 23.

29. Beattie, *Rediscovering Mary*, 26.

30. Mark Coleridge, *The Birth of the Lukan Narrative: Narrative as Christology in Luke 1–2* (Sheffield: Sheffield Academic Press, 1993), 77.

Notes

31. See Brant Pitre, *Jesus and the Jewish Roots of Mary* (New York: Image, 2018), 54–56.

32. René Laurentin, *The Truth of Christmas beyond the Myths* (Petersham, MA: St. Bede's Publications, 1986), 159. See also Barnabas M. Ahern, "The Infancy Narratives," in *A Voice Crying Out in the Desert*, ed. Carroll Stuhlmueller and Sebastian MacDonald (Collegeville, MN: Liturgical Press, 1996), 177. A somewhat different explanation is offered by Raymond E. Brown, *The Birth of the Messiah*, rev. ed. (New York: Doubleday, 1993), 344–45, and Marie E. Isaacs, "Mary in the Lucan Infancy Narrative," *The Way Supplement* 25 (1975): 94–95.

33. Duffy, *What Catholics Believe about Mary*, 7.

34. Joseph A. Fitzmyer, *The Gospel According to Luke I–IX* (New York: Doubleday, 1981), 359.

35. Lawrence Frizzell, "Mary's Magnificat, Sources and Themes," *Marian Studies* 50 (1999): 51. See also the fine comments on the Magnificat in Thomas G. Casey, *Mary in Different Traditions* (Mahwah, NJ: Paulist Press, 2020), 31.

36. Macquarrie, *Mary for All Christians*, 43.

37. Stephen Farris, *The Hymns of Luke's Infancy Narratives* (Sheffield: JSOT Press, 1985), 118.

38. Farris, *The Hymns of Luke's Infancy Narratives*, 122.

39. Shoemaker, *Mary in Early Christian Faith*, 34.

40. Pitre, *Jesus and the Jewish Roots of Mary*, 28. The other places in the Book of Genesis where Eve is called woman are 2:22, 23; 3:1, 2, 4, 6, 12, 13 (2x), 15, 16.

41. Gaventa, "Nothing Will Be Impossible," 20.

42. Lawrence Frizzell, "Mary and the Biblical Heritage," *Marian Studies* 46 (1995): 31.

43. de la Potterie, *Mary in the Mystery of the Covenant*, 219.

44. Preston, *Faces of the Church*, 252.

3. PATRISTIC MARY

1. John A. McGuckin, *The Westminster Handbook of Patristic Theology* (Louisville, KY: Westminster John Knox Press, 2004), 349.

2. Tina Beattie, "Mary in Patristic Theology," in *Mary: the Complete Resource*, ed. Sarah J. Boss (New York: Oxford University Press, 2007), 75.

3. John N. D. Kelly, *Early Christian Doctrines*, rev. ed. (Peabody, MA: Hendrickson Publishers, 2003), 491. I am much indebted to Kelly's masterful outline of Marian theology in this chapter.

4. Walter J. Burghardt, "Mary in Western Patristic Thought," in *Mariology*, ed. Juniper B. Carol, vol. 1 (Milwaukee: Bruce, 1955), 110. This outstanding essay by Burghardt is laced with multiple references to the fathers of the Church, texts not easily available to the average reader.

5. Kallistos Ware, "The Mother of God in Orthodox Theology and Devotion," in *Mary's Place in Christian Dialogue*, ed. Alberic Stacpoole (Wilton, CT: Morehouse-Barlow, 1982), 172.

6. In his *Dialogue with Trypho*, 100:4–6.; see Burghardt, "Mary in Western Patristic Thought," 111.

7. Burghardt, "Mary in Western Patristic Thought," 111.

8. *Against the Heresies* 5.19.1; see Burghardt, "Mary in Western Patristic Thought," 112.

9. Burghardt, "Mary in Western Patristic Thought," 117.

10. Hans von Campenhausen, *The Virgin Birth in the Theology of the Ancient Church* (Eugene, OR: Wipf and Stock, 2011), 22. Original English publication, 1954. The passages in Ignatius are *Ephesians* 7:2; 18:2; *Trallians* 9:1; *Smyrneans* 1:1.

11. See *1 Apology* 63:10; *2 Apology* 56:5; *Dialogue with Trypho*, 125.

12. See his *Dialogue with Trypho*, 48:4.

Notes

13. von Campenhausen, *The Virgin Birth*, 24–25. See *1 Apology* 21–22; 23:2–3; 54–55; *Dialogue with Trypho*, 69–70; 78:6.

14. In the same way as Justin, see also Irenaeus, *Against the Heresies* 4.33.4.

15. Ware, "The Mother of God," 170.

16. McGuckin, *Westminster Handbook of Patristic Theology*, 351.

17. Paul F. Palmer, *Mary in the Documents of the Church* (Westminster, MD: Newman, 1952), 53.

18. Norman P. Tanner, ed., *Decrees of the Ecumenical Councils*, vol. 1 (Washington, DC: Georgetown University Press, 1990), 59.

19. Burghardt, "Mary in Western Patristic Thought," 143.

20. *De natura et gratia* 36.42; see Burghardt, "Mary in Western Patristic Thought," 143.

21. Ware, "The Mother of God," 176–77.

22. Ware, "The Mother of God," 177–78.

23. Burghardt, "Mary in Western Patristic Thought," 148–49.

24. Burghardt, "Mary in Western Patristic Thought," 150.

25. William Dalrymple, *From the Holy Mountain* (New York: Henry Holt, 1997), 298.

26. Dalrymple, *From the Holy Mountain*, 299.

27. Andrew Louth, *St. John Damascene: Tradition and Originality in Byzantine Theology* (Oxford: Oxford University Press, 2002), 15.

28. Bernard McGinn, *Doctors of the Church: Thirty-Three Men and Women Who Shaped Christianity*, 2nd ed. (New York: Crossroad, 2009), 97.

29. Brian E. Daley, *On the Dormition of Mary: Early Patristic Homilies* (Crestwood, NY: St. Vladimir's Seminary Press, 1998), 21.

30. The three homilies are available in Daley, *On the Dormition of Mary*, 183–239.

31. See Daley, *On the Dormition of Mary*, 198.
32. See Daley, *On the Dormition of Mary*, 218.
33. See Daley, *On the Dormition of Mary*, 235.

4. SYRIAC MARY

1. Hugo Rahner, *Symbole der Kirche* (Salzburg: Otto Müller Verlag, 1964), 8, as cited in Robert Murray, *Symbols of Church and Kingdom: A Study in Early Syriac Tradition*, rev. ed. (New York: T. and T. Clark, 2006), 38.
2. Sebastian P. Brock, "Mary in Syriac Tradition," in *Mary's Place in Christian Dialogue*, ed. Alberic Stacpoole (Wilton, CT: Morehouse-Barlow, 1983), 182.
3. Murray, *Symbols of Church and Kingdom*, 1. The original edition was published by Cambridge University Press in 1975.
4. Murray, *Symbols of Church and Kingdom*, 185–86.
5. Murray, *Symbols of Church and Kingdom*, 188.
6. James H. Charlesworth, ed., *The Odes of Solomon* (Oxford: Clarendon Press, 1973), 81–82.
7. Miri Rubin, *Mother of God: A History of the Virgin Mary* (New Haven: Yale University Press, 2009), 37.
8. Murray, *Symbols of Church and Kingdom*, 31.
9. Kathleen McVey, *Ephrem the Syrian: Hymns* (New York: Paulist Press, 1989), 174–75.
10. Sebastian P. Brock, *The Luminous Eye: The Spiritual World Vision of St. Ephrem the Syrian* (Kalamazoo, MI: Cistercian Publications, 1992), 110.
11. See Carmel McCarthy, trans., "St. Ephrem's Commentary on Tatian's *Diatessaron*: An English Translation of Chester Beatty Syriac MS 709," *Journal of Semitic Studies Supplement* 2 (Oxford: Oxford University Press, 1993): 63.
12. See Brock, "Mary in Syriac Tradition," 184.

Notes

13. Brock, "Mary in Syriac Tradition," 185.
14. See Sebastian P. Brock, "Introduction," in *Jacob of Serug*, trans. Mary Hansbury (Crestwood, NY: St. Vladimir's Seminary Press, 1998), 8.

5. CELTIC MARY

1. Richard P. C. Hanson, *Saint Patrick: His Origins and Career* (Oxford: Clarendon Press, 1968), 205.
2. Thomas O'Loughlin, *Saint Patrick: The Man and His Works* (London: SPCK, 1999), 2, 9.
3. O'Loughlin, *Saint Patrick*, 4.
4. See, e.g., Owen F. Cummings, "Lenten Saints: Patrick and Joseph," *The Priest* 70 (2014): 47–52.
5. The *Stowe Missal* is so-called because it once belonged to a collection of manuscripts that had been owned by the Marquis of Buckingham of Stowe House.
6. Following Thomas O'Loughlin, *Celtic Theology* (New York: Continuum, 2000), 128–30.
7. O'Loughlin, *Celtic Theology*, 130.
8. O'Loughlin, *Celtic Theology*, 138.
9. Esther de Waal, *The Celtic Vision* (London: Darton, Longman and Todd, 1988).
10. de Waal, *Celtic Vision*, 4.
11. de Waal, *Celtic Vision*, 5–8.
12. de Waal, *Celtic Vision*, 10, 175, 186.
13. For an introduction to John Macquarrie's theology, see Owen F. Cummings, *John Macquarrie, Master of Theology*, intro. by Rev. Prof. John Macquarrie (Mahwah, NJ: Paulist Press, 2002).
14. See especially Alan Macquarrie, *The Saints of Scotland* (Edinburgh: John Donald, 1997).

15. John Macquarrie, "Mary and the Saints in Early Scottish Poetry," in *Mary for Earth and Heaven: Essays on Mary and Ecumenism*, ed. William McLoughlin and Jill Pinnock (Leominster, UK: Gracewing, 2002), 380.

16. See Macquarrie, "Mary and the Saints in Early Scottish Poetry," 382.

17. Macquarrie, "Mary and the Saints in Early Scottish Poetry," 385.

6. MUSLIM MARY

1. Timothy Winter, "Mary in Islam," in *Mary, The Complete Resource*, ed. Sarah Jane Boss (Oxford: Oxford University Press, 2017), 479. This fine essay by Winter goes on to give examples of Muslim interest in Mary not only from the Qur'an, but from medieval and modern Muslim literature.

2. R. J. McCarthy, "Mary in Islam," in *Mary's Place in Christian Dialogue*, ed. Alberic Stacpoole (Wilton, CT: Morehouse-Barlow, 1983), 202. I am much indebted to this fine essay by Fr. McCarthy.

3. Miri Rubin, *Mother of God: A History of the Virgin Mary* (New Haven: Yale University Press, 2009), 83.

4. Thomas G. Casey, *Mary in Different Traditions* (Mahwah, NJ: Paulist Press, 2020), 74.

5. Ninian Smart, *The Religious Experience of Mankind* (New York: Charles Scribner's Sons, 1969), 480.

6. *Sura* 4:169–70, 171–72.

7. *The Infancy Gospel of Thomas* 2:1–7, in *The Complete Gospels: Annotated Scholars Version*, ed. Robert J. Miller, 3rd ed. (San Francisco: Harper San Francisco, 1992), 371.

8. Hans Küng, Josef van Ess, Heinrich von Stietencron, and Heinz Bechert, *Christianity and the World Religions* (New York: Doubleday, 1986), 124–25.

Notes

9. Vatican II, "Declaration on the Relationship of Christianity to World Religions," in *The Documents of Vatican II*, ed. Walter M. Abbott and Joseph Gallagher (New York: America Press, 1966).
10. Winter, "Mary in Islam," 479.
11. Cited in Jacques Jomier, *How to Understand Islam* (New York: Crossroad, 1991), 66.
12. McCarthy, "Mary in Islam," 203.
13. The texts may be found in the highly respected translation of A. J. Arberry, *The Koran Interpreted* (London: Allen and Unwin, 1955).
14. Winter, "Mary in Islam," 480, writes, "While it is impossible to propose a genealogy for the Qur'an's Marian passages, it has long been recognized that these not only share some of the motifs and concerns of the canonical infancy narratives, but also resonate with the most important extra canonical source of Marian narratives, the *Protoevangelium of James*."
15. See, e.g., *Sura* 5:116.
16. Rubin, *Mother of God*, 87.
17. See her *The Misunderstood Jew* (Harper San Francisco, 2006). Levine teaches at Vanderbilt University, and according to the Vanderbilt website, in spring 2019 she was the first Jew to teach New Testament at Rome's Pontifical Biblical Institute.
18. McCarthy, "Mary in Islam," 210–11.

7. MEDIEVAL MARY

1. David N. Bell, *Many Mansions: An Introduction to the Development and Diversity of Medieval Theology* (Kalamazoo, MI: Cistercian Publications, 1996), 263–64.
2. This crisp summary comes from "The Seattle Statement, Mary: Grace and Hope in Christ," in *Mary: Grace and*

Hope in Christ, ed. Donald Bolen and Gregory Cameron (New York: Continuum, 2006), 45–47.

3. Luigi Gambero, *Mary in the Middle Ages* (San Francisco: Ignatius Press, 2005), 131.

4. Bernard of Clairvaux, *Sermon on the Nativity of Blessed Mary,* 7, cited in Bell, *Many Mansions,* 252–53.

5. Bell, *Many Mansions,* 257.

6. Gambero, *Mary in the Middle Ages,* 135.

7. Hilda Graef, *Mary: A History of Doctrine and Devotion,* combined edition (Westminster, MD: Christian Classics, 1985), 236.

8. Graef, *Mary: A History,* 236.

9. Cited in Gambero, *Mary in the Middle Ages,* 138.

10. Gambero, *Mary in the Middle Ages,* 235.

11. Gambero, *Mary in the Middle Ages,* 238.

12. St. Thomas Aquinas, *Summa Theologiae* III, q. 27, a. 2.

13. Graef, *Mary: A History,* 302.

14. Consider these words of Michael O'Carroll in his article "Mary, Mother of God," in *The New Dictionary of Theology,* ed. Joseph Komonchak, Mary Collins and Dermot A. Lane (Collegeville, MN: Liturgical Press, 1987), 640: "But it was Duns Scotus who breached the opposition wall: Mary could be redeemed by preservation, still due to Christ, as all others are by liberation."

15. Bolen and Cameron, *Mary: Grace and Hope,* 47.

8. MARY AND THE REFORMERS

1. George Tavard, *The Thousand Faces of the Blessed Virgin* (Collegeville, MN: Liturgical Press, 1996), 126.

2. Christopher O'Donnell, "Mary and Ecumenism: Paths Ahead," in *Reconciliation,* ed. Oliver Rafferty (Dublin: Columba Press, 1993), 80.

Notes

3. Kenneth Clark, *Civilization: A Personal View* (New York: Harper and Row, 1969), 159.

4. Thomas A. O'Meara, *Mary in Protestant and Catholic Theology* (New York: Sheed and Ward, 1966), 113. O'Meara refers in his endnotes not only to Luther's own work but also to established Lutheran commentators. O'Meara's references are to the classic German edition of Luther's works: *Weimarer Ausgabe*, abbreviated as WA, 57 volumes (Berlin: Walter de Gruyter, 1931–44).

5. Walter J. Hollenweger, "Ave Maria: Mary, the Reformers and the Protestants," *One in Christ* 13 (1977): 287.

6. Gottfried Maron, "Mary in Protestant Theology," in *Mary in the Churches*, ed. Hans Küng and Jürgen Moltmann (New York: Seabury Press, 1983), 41.

7. WA 1, 61, 77–79, cited in O'Meara, *Mary in Protestant and Catholic Theology*, 116.

8. Martin Luther, *Commentary on the Magnificat* (St. Louis: Concordia Press, 1960) 34, as cited in O'Meara, *Mary in Protestant and Catholic Theology*, 117.

9. Thomas G. Casey, *Mary in Different Traditions* (Mahwah, NJ: Paulist Press, 2020), 14.

10. Casey, *Mary in Different Traditions*, 10.

11. Diarmaid MacCulloch, "Mary and Sixteenth-Century Protestants," in *The Church and Mary*, ed. R. N. Swanson (Rochester, NY: 2004), 201.

12. O'Meara, *Mary in Protestant and Catholic Theology*, 124. Consider also the comment of Thomas G. Casey, SJ, in his *Mary in Different Traditions* (Mahwah, NJ: Paulist Press, 2020), 7: "After (the deaths of the great reformers) from the late sixteenth century onward, attitudes toward Mary took a downward turn among most of the Reformed churches. The sole exception was the Church of England. To this day, the Virgin Mary continues to be held in high esteem by Anglicans."

13. O'Meara, *Mary in Protestant and Catholic Theology*, 125.
14. Hollenweger, "Ave Maria," 288.
15. Maron, "Mary in Protestant Theology," 41–42.
16. MacCulloch, "Mary and Sixteenth-Century Protestants," 196.
17. Zwingli is thus paraphrased in Hollenweger, "Ave Maria," 288.
18. Maron, "Mary in Protestant Theology," 46.
19. Beverly R. Gaventa, *Mary: Glimpses of the Mother of Jesus* (Columbia: University of South Carolina Press, 1995), 18.
20. John Macquarrie, *Principles of Christian Theology*, 2nd ed. (New York: Scribner's, 1977), 393. A helpful situating of Macquarrie on the map of ecumenical Mariology may be found in Donal Flanagan, "Mary and the Unremembered Past," *Doctrine and Life* 43 (1993): 259–66.
21. See Paul Williams, "The Virgin Mary in Anglican Tradition," in *Mary: The Complete Resource*, ed. Sarah Jane Boss (New York: Oxford University Press, 2007), 314–15.
22. Published originally in *Holy Cross Magazine*, May 1966.
23. Macquarrie, *Principles of Christian Theology*, 395.
24. *Principles of Christian Theology*, 392.
25. *Principles of Christian Theology*, 395.
26. *Principles of Christian Theology*, 396.
27. *Principles of Christian Theology*, 397.
28. *Principles of Christian Theology*, 394; see also Macquarrie, *Mary for All Christians*, 46–47.
29. Macquarrie, *Principles of Christian Theology*, 395.
30. David Carter, "Mary in Ecumenical Dialogue and Exchange," in *Mary: The Complete Resource*, ed. Sarah Jane Boss (New York: Oxford University Press, 2007), 341.

Notes

9. MARY IN VATICAN II'S CONSTITUTION ON THE CHURCH

1. Eamon Duffy, *What Catholics Believe about Mary* (London: Catholic Truth Society, 1989), 4.
2. Christopher O'Donnell, "Mary and the Church," in his *Ecclesia: A Theological Encyclopedia of the Church* (Collegeville, MN: Liturgical Press, 1996), 291.
3. O'Donnell, "Mary and the Church," 291–92.
4. O'Donnell, "Mary and the Church," 292.
5. See Christopher O'Donnell, "Mary and Ecumenism, Paths Ahead," in *Reconciliation: Essays in Honour of Michael Hurley*, ed. Oliver Rafferty (Dublin: The Columba Press, 1993), 80–97.
6. Stefano De Fiores, "Mary in Postconciliar Theology," in *Vatican II: Assessment and Perspectives*, vol. 1, ed. Rene Latourelle, SJ (New York: Paulist Press, 1988), 471. To illustrate something of what De Fiores is getting at one might turn to the observation of the established Irish Marian scholar Donald Flanagan: "The recorded statements of Pope Pius XII on the Blessed Virgin out-bulk the combined contributions of his five predecessors." See his "The Blessed Virgin Mary, Mother of God, in the Mystery of Christ and the Church," in *The Church: A Theological and Pastoral Commentary on the Constitution on the Church*, ed. Kevin McNamara (Dublin: Veritas Publications, 1983), 318. See also H. E. Cardinale, "Pope Pius XII and the Blessed Virgin Mary," in *Mary's Place in Christian Dialogue*, ed. Alberic Stacpoole (Wilton, CT: Morehouse-Barlow, 1982), 248–60.
7. O'Donnell, "Mary and the Church," 292.
8. Robert W. Jenson, "A Space for God," in *Mary Mother of God*, ed. Carl. E. Braaten and Robert W. Jenson (Grand Rapids, MI: Eerdmans, 2004), 56.

9. David S. Yeago, "The Presence of Mary in the Mystery of the Church," in Braaten and Jenson, eds., *Mary Mother of God*, 59.

10. See Owen F. Cummings, *One Body in Christ: Ecumenical Snapshots* (Eugene, OR: Pickwick Publications/Wipf and Stock, 2015), 82–94, offering an example from Methodist theologian and patristic scholar Frances Young.

10. THE MARIAN DOGMAS

1. Christopher O'Donnell, "Mary and Ecumenism," in *Reconciliation*, ed. Oliver Rafferty (Dublin: The Columba Press, 1993), 82.
2. Herbert McCabe, *God Matters* (London: Geoffrey Chapman, 1987), 210.
3. St. Augustine, *On Nature and Grace*, 36.42.
4. Daniel E. Doyle, "Mary, Mother of God," in *Augustine through the Ages: An Encyclopedia*, ed. Allan D. Fitzgerald (Grand Rapids, MI: Eerdmans, 1999), 544.
5. *Summa Theologiae* III, q. 27, a. 2, ad 4.
6. Vladimir Lossky, *The Mystical Theology of the Eastern Church* (London: James Clarke, 1957), 140.
7. John Macquarrie, *Mary for All Christians* (Grand Rapids, MI: Eerdmans, 1990), 54.
8. In this section I will be following closely the contribution of John Macquarrie in chap. 3 of his *Mary for All Christians*.
9. Macquarrie, *Mary for All Christians*, 62.
10. Macquarrie, *Mary for All Christians*, 63.
11. Macquarrie, *Mary for All Christians*, 65–66. See also in this respect the fine comments of Thomas G. Casey, *Mary in Different Traditions* (Mahwah, NJ: Paulist Press, 2020), 49–72.
12. Macquarrie, *Mary for All Christians*, 68.

Notes

13. Macquarrie, *Mary for All Christians*, 70.
14. Macquarrie, *Mary for All Christians*, 71.
15. Macquarrie, *Mary for All Christians*, 71–72.
16. Anthony Tambasco, *What Are They Saying About Mary?* (New York: Paulist Press, 1984), 50.
17. John Macquarrie, *Principles of Christian Theology*, rev. ed. (New York: Harper, 1977), 398.
18. Macquarrie, *Mary for All Christians*, 81–82. See also the very favorable comments on Macquarrie's understanding of the assumption of Mary in Matthew Levering, *Mary's Bodily Assumption* (Notre Dame, IN: University of Notre Dame Press, 2015), 151–52.
19. As cited in Macquarrie, *Mary for All Christians*, 84.
20. Macquarrie, *Mary for All Christians*, 91. Eamon Duffy writes in a similar vein: "The Assumption is therefore important not for its uniqueness, nor as the final event in the terrestrial biography of Mary, but as an eschatological sign and promise of the glorious destiny of all the children of God—we shall all, in God's time, be assumed into heaven." See Eamon Duffy, *What Catholics Believe About Mary* (London: Catholic Truth Society, 1989), 17.
21. Casey, *Mary in Different Traditions*, 71.

11. AT THE SCHOOL OF MARY, "WOMAN OF THE EUCHARIST"

1. English translation, Pope John Paul II, *On the Eucharist* (Washington, DC: United States Conference of Catholic Bishops, 2003). All numerical references are to the text of the encyclical itself.
2. Aidan Nichols, "Rediscovering the Holy Sacrifice," *The Catholic Herald*, April 25, 2003.

3. See Charlene Spretnak, *Missing Mary* (New York: Palgrave Macmillan, 2004). There are many good things in this book, but I find the author's criticism of Vatican II excessive and, in some degree, ideological.

4. Tina Beattie, *Rediscovering Mary: Insights from the Gospels* (Liguori, MO: Triumph Books, 1995), 21–23.

5. See John Drury, *Painting the Word: Christian Pictures and Their Meanings* (New Haven: Yale University Press, 1999), 43–45.

6. Joseph Ratzinger, *God Is Near Us* (San Francisco: Ignatius Press, 2003), 24.

7. Cited in A. M. Allchin, *The Joy of All Creation* (Cambridge, MA: Cowley Publications, 1984), 131.

8. Edwin Muir, *An Autobiography*, reprint ed. (New York: Farrar, Strauss and Giroux, 1990), 228.

9. Peter H. Butter, ed., *Selected Letters of Edwin Muir* (New York: Random House, 1974), 278.

10. Archbishop Rowan D. Williams, "Sermon on the Occasion of the National Pilgrimage to the Shrine of Our Lady of Walsingham," Monday, May 31, 2004, 1–2.

11. Bernard of Clairvaux, *In laudibus Virginis Mariae*, Homily 4.8.

12. See Warren Dicharry, *Praying the Rosary* (Collegeville, MN: Liturgical Press, 1998), 4–6.

13. Williams, "Sermon," 1.

14. George Lindbeck, "Augsburg and the *Ecclesia de Eucharistia*," *Pro Ecclesia* 12 (2003): 411.

12. PRAYING THE ROSARY

1. Eamon Duffy, *Faith of Our Fathers* (New York: Continuum, 2004), 29.

Notes

2. Andrew M. Greeley, *The Catholic Imagination* (Berkeley: University of California Press, 2000), 1, 77–78.

3. Paul Moyaert, "In Defense of Praying with Images," *American Catholic Philosophical Quarterly* 81 (2007): 612. I owe this reference to my philosopher-son, Dr. Andrew Cummings.

4. George Tavard, *The Thousand Faces of the Virgin Mary* (Collegeville, MN: Liturgical Press, 1996), 94.

5. Pope John Paul II, *Apostolic Letter on the Most Holy Rosary* (Rome: Vatican City Press, 2002), 1, 36. See also the helpful commentary of Peter Casarella, "Contemplating Christ through the Eyes of Mary," *Pro Ecclesia* 14 (2005): 161–73.

6. Pope John Paul II, *Apostolic Letter on the Most Holy Rosary*, 2.

7. Timothy Radcliffe, "The Rosary," in his *Sing a New Song* (Springfield, IL: Templegate, 1999), 295.

8. In Bob Hurd, Elaine Park, and Charles Rohrbacher, *A Contemplative Rosary* (Portland: Oregon Catholic Press, 2004), 18.

9. Hurd, Park, and Rohrbacher, *Contemplative Rosary*, 19.

10. This theme is found throughout Meister Eckhart. See, e.g., Sermon 24, in *Meister Eckhart: Selected Writings*, ed. Oliver Davies (New York: Penguin, 1995), 215–22.

11. Nuala O'Faolain, *Are You Somebody?* (New York: Holt Paperbacks, 2009), 98.

12. Pope John Paul II, *Apostolic Letter on the Most Holy Rosary*, 21.

13. Timothy Radcliffe, *What Is the Point of Being a Christian?* (New York: Continuum, 2005), 96.

13. MARY TODAY

1. Thomas G. Casey, *Mary in Different Traditions* (Mahwah, NJ: Paulist Press, 2020), 86.

2. John Macquarrie, *Mary for All Christians* (Grand Rapids, MI: Eerdmans, 1991), 16.

3. Casey, *Mary in Different Traditions*, 5. See Seamus Heaney, "Like Everybody Else," in his *District and Circle* (New York: Farrar, Straus and Giroux, 2006), 45.

4. Macquarrie, *Mary for All Christians*, 116–35.

5. Macquarrie, *Mary for All Christians*, 120.

6. Eamon Duffy, "May Thoughts on Mary," in *Faith of Our Fathers* (New York: Continuum, 2004), 29.

7. Duffy, "May Thoughts on Mary," 29.

8. Duffy, "May Thoughts on Mary," 33.

9. Duffy, "May Thoughts on Mary," 34–35.

10. Duffy, "May Thoughts on Mary," 35.

11. Eamon Duffy, *What Catholics Believe about Mary* (London: Catholic Truth Society, 1989), 3.

12. Duffy, *What Catholics Believe about Mary*, 4.

13. Herbert McCabe, *God Matters* (London: Geoffrey Chapman, 1987), 211. McCabe's comment is made with reference to the immaculate conception, but it could be applied more generally as we are doing here to the sweep of the Marian tradition of devotion and reflection.

14. Duffy, *What Catholics Believe About Mary*, 19.

BIBLIOGRAPHY

Beattie, Tina. "Mary in Patristic Theology." In *Mary, the Complete Resource*, edited by Sarah J. Boss, 75–105. New York and Oxford: Oxford University Press, 2007.
———. *Rediscovering Mary: Insights from the Gospels*. Liguori, MO: Triumph Books, 1995.
Bell, David N. *Many Mansions: An Introduction to the Development and Diversity of Medieval Theology*. Collegeville, MN: Liturgical Press/Cistercian Publications, 2008.
Burghardt, Walter J. "Mary in Western Patristic Thought." In *Mariology*, vol. 1, edited by Juniper B. Carol, 109–55. Milwaukee: Bruce, 1955.
Carr, Anne. "Mary, Model of Faith." In *Mary, Woman for Today*, edited by Doris Donnelly, 7–24. New York: Paulist Press, 1990.
Carter, David. "Mary in Ecumenical Dialogue and Exchange." In *Mary, the Complete Resource*, edited by Sarah Jane Boss, 340–60. New York: Oxford University Press, 2007.
Casey, Thomas G. *Mary in Different Traditions*. Mahwah, NJ: Paulist Press, 2020.
Cummings, Owen F. "The Historical Mary of Nazareth." *The Priest* 48 (1992): 14–17.
———. "Lenten Saints: Patrick and Joseph." *The Priest* 70 (2014): 47–52.

———. *Thinking about Prayer*. Eugene, OR: Wipf and Stock, 2009.
Cunningham, Lawrence S. "Born of a Woman (Gal. 4:4): A Theological Meditation." In *Mary Mother of God*, edited by Carl E. Braaten and Robert W Jenson, 36–48. Grand Rapids, MI: Eerdmans, 2004.
De Fiores, Stefano. "Mary in Postconciliar Theology." In *Vatican II: Assessment and Perspectives*, vol. 1, edited by Rene Latourelle, 469–539. New York: Paulist Press, 1988.
de Waal, Esther. *The Celtic Vision*. London: Darton, Longman and Todd, 1988.
Donnelly, Doris, ed. *Mary, Woman of Nazareth*. New York: Paulist Press, 1989.
Duffy, Eamon. *Faith of Our Fathers*. New York: Continuum, 2004.
———. *What Catholics Believe about Mary*. London: Catholic Truth Society, 1989.
Flanagan, Donal. "The Blessed Virgin Mary, Mother of God, in the Mystery of Christ and the Church." In *The Church: A Theological and Pastoral Commentary on the Constitution on the Church*, edited by Kevin McNamara, 317–56. Dublin: Veritas Publications, 1983.
Gaventa, Beverly. *Mary: Glimpses of the Mother of Jesus*. Columbia: University of Southern Carolina Press, 1995.
———. "'Nothing Will Be Impossible with God,' Mary as the Mother of Believers." In *Mary Mother of God*, edited by Carl E. Braaten and Robert W. Jenson, 19–35. Grand Rapids, MI: Eerdmans, 2004.
Gebara, Ivone, and Maria C. Bingemer. *Mary Mother of God, Mother of the Poor*. Maryknoll, NY: Orbis Books, 1989.
George, Timothy. "The Blessed Virgin Mary in Evangelical Perspective." In *Mary Mother of God*, edited by Carl E. Braaten and Robert W. Jenson, 100–122. Grand Rapids, MI: Eerdmans, 2004.

Bibliography

Greeley, Andrew M. *The Catholic Imagination*. Berkeley: University of California Press, 2000.

Green, Joel B. "Blessed Is She Who Believed." In *Blessed One: Protestant Perspectives on Mary*, edited by Beverly R. Gaventa and Cynthia L. Rigby, 9–20. Louisville, KY: Westminster John Knox Press, 2002.

Hanson, Richard P. C. *Saint Patrick, His Origins and Career*. Oxford: Clarendon Press, 1968.

Hollenweger, Walter J. "Ave Maria: Mary, the Reformers and the Protestants," *One in Christ* 13 (1977).

Ilan, Tai. "Women in Jewish Life and Law." In *The Cambridge History of Judaism*, vol. 4, edited by Steven T. Katz, 628. Cambridge: Cambridge University Press, 2006.

Jenson, Robert W. "A Space for God." In *Mary Mother of God*, edited by Carl E. Braaten and Robert W. Jenson, 49–57. Grand Rapids, MI: Eerdmans, 2004.

Johnson, Elizabeth A., *Truly Our Sister: A Theology of Mary in the Communion of Saints*. New York and London: Continuum, 2003.

Küng, Hans, Josef van Ess, Heinrich von Stietencron, and Heinz Bechert. *Christianity and the World Religions*. New York: Doubleday, 1986.

Lange, Nicholas de. "A Woman in Israel." In *Mary and the Churches*, edited by Alberic Stacpoole, 192–201. Slough: St. Paul Publications, 1982.

MacCulloch, Diarmaid. "Mary and Sixteenth Century Protestants." In *The Church and Mary*, edited by R. N. Swanson. Rochester, NY and Woodbridge, UK: The Boydell Press, 2004.

Macquarrie, Alan. *The Saints of Scotland*. Edinburgh: John Donald, 1997.

Macquarrie, John. "Mary and the Saints in Early Scottish Poetry." In *Mary for Earth and Heaven: Essays on Mary* and *Ecumenism*, edited by William McLoughlin and Jill Pinnock. Leominster, UK: Gracewing, 2002.

———. *Principles of Christian Theology*, rev. ed. New York: Scribner's Sons, 1977.

Maron, Gottfied. "Mary in Protestant Theology." In *Mary in the Churches*, edited by Hans Küng and Jürgen Moltmann. New York: The Seabury Press, 1983.

Maunder, Chris. "Mary in the New Testament and Apocrypha." In *Mary: The Complete Resource*, edited by Sarah Jane Boss, 11–46. New York: Oxford University Press, 2007.

McCabe, Herbert. *God Matters*. London: Geoffrey Chapman, 1987.

McGuckin, John A. *The Westminster Handbook of Patristic Theology*. Louisville, KY: Westminster John Knox Press, 2004.

McKenzie, John L. "The Mother of Jesus in the New Testament." In *Mary in the Churches*, edited by Hans Küng and Jurgen Moltmann, 3–11. New York: Herder and Herder, 1983.

Moyaert, Paul. "In Defense of Praying with Images," *American Catholic Philosophical Quarterly* 81 (2007): 595–612.

O'Carroll, Michael. "Mary, Mother of God." In *The New Dictionary of Theology*, edited by Joseph Komonchak, Mary Collins, and Dermot A. Lane, 637–43. Collegeville, MN: Liturgical Press, 1987.

O'Donnell, Christopher. "Mary and the Church," in *Ecclesia: An Encyclopedia of the Church*, 291–93. Collegeville, MN: Liturgical Press, 1996.

———. "Mary and Ecumenism: Paths Ahead." In *Reconciliation*, edited by Oliver Rafferty, 80–97. Dublin: Columba Press, 1993.

O'Loughlin, Thomas. *Celtic Theology*. New York: Continuum, 2000.

Bibliography

———. *Saint Patrick: The Man and His Works*. London: SPCK, 1999.
O'Meara, Thomas A. *Mary in Protestant and Catholic Theology*. New York: Sheed and Ward, 1966.
Pitre, Brant. *Jesus and the Jewish Roots of Mary*. New York: Image, 2018.
Rubin, Miri. *Mother of God: A History of the Virgin Mary*. New Haven: Yale University Press. 2009.
Senior, Donald. "Gospel Portrait of Mary: Images and Symbols from the Synoptic Tradition." In *Mary: Woman of Nazareth*, edited by Doris Donnelly, 92–108. New York: Paulist Press, 1989.
Shoemaker, Stephen J. *Mary in Early Christian Faith and Devotion*. New Haven: Yale University Press, 2016.
Tavard, George. *The Thousand Faces of the Virgin Mary*. Collegeville, MN: Liturgical Press, 1996.
Vermes, Geza. *Jesus and the World of Judaism*. London: SCM Press, 1983.
———. "Miriam the Jewess," *The Way Supplement* 45 (1982): 55–64.
Ware, Kallistos. "The Mother of God in Orthodox Theology and Devotion." In *Mary's Place in Christian Dialogue*, edited by Alberic Stacpoole, 169–81. Wilton, CT: Morehouse-Barlow, 1982.
Williams, Paul. "The Virgin Mary in the Anglican Tradition." In *Mary: The Complete Resource*, edited by Sarah Jane Boss, 314–39. Oxford: Oxford University Press, 2007.
Winter, Timothy. "Mary in Islam." In *Mary: The Complete Resource*, edited by Sarah Jane Boss, 479–502. New York: Oxford University Press, 2007.
Yeago, David S. "The Presence of Mary in the Mystery of the Church." In *Mary Mother of God*, edited by Carl E. Braaten and Robert W. Jenson, 58–79. Grand Rapids, MI: Eerdmans, 2004.

www.ingramcontent.com/pod-product-compliance
Lightning Source LLC
Chambersburg PA
CBHW070553160426
43199CB00014B/2482